MIRACLE
factor

MIRACLE
factor

Awesome Stories of Satellite Evangelism

Kandus Thorp

Pacific Press® Publishing Association
Nampa, Idaho
Oshawa, Ontario, Canada
www.pacificpress.com

Design by Darrin Brooks
It Is Written Digital Media Group
Cover photo illustration by Darrin Brooks; satellite image by Corbis.

Channels is a publication of the It Is Written television ministry.
Stories from this magazine are used with permission.

Additional copies of this book are available by calling toll free
1-800-765-6955 or by visiting <http://www.adventistbookcenter.com>.

ISBN: 0-8163-2501-1

05 06 07 08 09 • 5 4 3 2 1

Dedication

Jonathon, Chris, and Stephen
I am so proud of you!
Positions, titles, and service change,
Details: inconsequential.
Oceans separate friends,
Life goes on . . .

I will always be your mom.

I look forward to eternity,
Together:
Friends and family,
Dad,
and each of you.

I love you!

Table of Contents

Forewords

Since we have been told that the "last movements on earth will be rapid ones," we shouldn't be surprised by the speed with which the Advent movement has embraced satellite technology. Through God's blessing, the Seventh-day Adventist Church has used satellite evangelism to great benefit. The church has now also moved into the exciting worldwide evangelistic outreach of Adventist programming on a twenty-four-hour-per-day, seven-days-per-week, "direct-to-home" basis through the Hope channels.

God's miraculous hand is very much evident in this fast-paced expansion of the Adventist Television Network (ATN). Although satellite technology itself does not convert people, the Holy Spirit has been using ATN and the Hope channels effectively to lift up Christ and reach hearts around the world with the precious Adventist message and the proclamation of Revelation 14.

Miracle Factor recounts God's miracles in the use of this new technology for soul winning and how God uses individuals and technology to point people to Jesus and His soon coming. As you read this book, rejoice with the thousands who have accepted the Advent message through ATN activities, and pray for this greatly expanding evangelistic outreach in its attempt to glorify God by bringing His truth and hope into as many homes and churches as possible around the globe.

Pastor Ted N. C. Wilson, Chair
Adventist Television Network Operating Committee, and General Vice
President General Conference of Seventh-day Adventists

You are holding in your hands a chronicle of miracles. This is the modern-day book of Acts repeated.

In 1995, for the very first time, the Seventh-day Adventist Church up-linked via satellite God's last-day message. I still remember the thrill of standing on the stage of the Chattanooga Convention Center, sensing that God was powerfully at work. Think of it: The gospel traveled twenty-four thousand miles to a satellite receiver, was relayed another twenty-four thousand miles back to earth—and the entire process took less than a second as eager viewers anxiously awaited the truth of God's Word to descend from the sky!

In *Miracle Factor,* you will read story after story of God's opening incredible doors to spread His message to the world via satellite. There are stories of amazing sacrifice that will bring you to tears. There are sagas of unwavering faith that will inspire you to dedicate yourself anew. There are incidents of providential intervention that will leave you awestruck with wonder at our great God.

Kandus Thorp is well qualified to share these miracles of faith. Along with her husband, Brad, who serves as director of Adventist Television Network and the Hope Channels, she has participated in more than eighty satellite uplink events, witnessing the baptism of hundreds of thousands as a result. Kandus writes not from a detached distance but passionately from the front lines of satellite evangelism.

The three angels' messages are streaming across the sky via satellite and being downlinked to thatch-roofed huts in Ghana, tenement apartment complexes in the Bronx, million-dollar condominiums in Rio de Janeiro, and cinder-block churches in Nairobi. From Los Angeles to London, Lagos to Lahore, God's Word is proclaimed. The truth has taken wing and is flying in midheaven.

Catch the vision. Experience the thrill. Share the inspiration of the men and women on the cutting edge of an evangelistic breakthrough for our day. This is their story. The story of ordinary people who dared to dream, who courageously forged ahead against criticism and obstacles, who believed God would move mightily—and He did.

There is only one problem with this book: When you begin reading it, you won't be able to put it down. But that's all right, because God's glory shines through on every page.

Mark A. Finley, Field Secretary
General Conference of Seventh-day Adventists

Miracles are miracles. Don't try to understand them; you will never do it. If you could understand them, they would stop being miracles. You must accept them, not question them. That is more relevant when we are talking about divine miracles.

Miracle Factor is the telling of God's prodigious acts, the wonders that He has done in the lives of many people around the world through the wonderful ministry of television—people who felt confused or lost in life due to random circumstances, people who were looking everywhere and couldn't find a way out, people who were facing struggles that were unbearable when suddenly God's Spirit reached them with the good news of the gospel. These people just had to let the Spirit move and their night became bright as day. The sun started to shine in the midst of darkness, and today they are living proof of God's love and ever-transforming power.

I'm sure that as you read this book, you will be deeply moved. I pray that you come to realize that miracles can't be explained, but only accepted.

Pastor Alejandro Bullón, Director
South American Division Ministerial Association
General Conference of Seventh-day Adventists

Introduction

How do you tell a million stories?

How do you tell the miraculous way God has guided the Adventist Church through satellite evangelism to establish a global television network of Hope channels that are currently broadcasting full time to various regions of the world?

The start, growth, development, and now the rapid spread of Adventist Television Network (ATN) around the world is clearly the result of God's miraculous leading. Time after time in satellite NET evangelism, we have seen God perform miracles on behalf of this innovative technique for sharing the gospel. The divine confirmation has moved church leaders to give increasingly stronger support. It has motivated hundreds of thousands of church members in thousands of churches to sacrifice boldly and work as united teams to build this television network for spreading the gospel.

Until now, the story of ATN and its Hope Channels has been one of the untold miracle stories in a modern book of Acts. Since the first satellite NET event in 1995 with the Adventist Communication Network (ACN) in North America, satellite evangelism has been a huge blessing. More than one million people are reported to have been baptized into the world Adventist Church family at least in part through the influence of this ministry.

Miracle Factor isn't a chronological history. This book doesn't focus on committees and their deliberations. It doesn't tell the stories of all the individuals and organizations that have contributed to satellite evangelism. *Miracle Factor* focuses on the miraculous acts of God—on how God has providentially guided and intervened in establishing ATN, Hope Channel ministry. As you read these stories, you may wonder how the word "miracle" is defined and used. The following explanation may be helpful to you.

What is a miracle?

There's the miracle of conversion—God's greatest miracle, that of transforming the human heart. John 3 records Jesus' statement that each of us must be "born again." The conversion of more than one million precious people represents a miracle of God.

There's the miracle of the extraordinary. When people die, they don't normally come back to life. Those who are lame, blind, or deaf from birth normally aren't healed. But Jesus raised the dead and healed the lame, blind, and deaf. At times, God works in extraordinary ways.

At ATN, we strongly believe in good management and proper planning. We do our best to prepare for the satellite evangelism events in which we're involved. However, the best-laid plans of human beings often go astray. At critical times, the ATN staff have found themselves in circumstances that demanded divine intervention if success was to be had. And God does work in extraordinary ways. Burnt-out PA amplifiers do not ordinarily work properly and amplify sound. Without a generator or some other power source, electrical power does not ordinarily flow to a city block and a church when the entire city has lost electrical power. Yet in the following pages you will read stories of these things happening in response to the prayers of God's people. These extraordinary happenings represent divine miracles.

Then there's the miracle of the "right answer." Luke 12:10–12; 21:14, 15 records Jesus' promise to send the Holy Spirit to guide us into all truth and to provide answers and wisdom when adversaries or difficult situations confront us. God places people in positions and circumstances to give solutions. Although possibly not as dramatic as the "extraordinary" miracles, this guidance is no less a divine miracle. Some of the following stories relate these "miracles of the right answer."

As you enter the world of satellite evangelism through this book, Kandus's and my hope and prayer is that your confidence in our Almighty God will be strengthened. We hope you will be inspired to a deeper prayer experience. Our goal is that you will be encouraged to do greater and bolder things for God.

Brad Thorp, Director
Adventist Television Network
Hope Channel

Getting Started—
NET '95

Your ways, O God, are holy.
  What god is so great as our God?
You are the God who performs miracles;
  you display your power among the peoples.—Psalm 77:13, 14, NIV

In the spring of 1993, the telephone rang in our home office. "Brad, would you be willing to coordinate the preparation across North America for NET '95?" asked Pastor Glenn Aufderhar, president of the Adventist Media Center in California.

"What is 'NET '95'?" my husband, Brad, responded.

Pastor Aufderhar explained the bold new plan of the North American Adventist Church to broadcast via satellite an evangelistic series presented by Mark Finley, speaker/director of the It Is Written television ministry. For the initiative to succeed, churches would have to be convinced of the concept's potential and buy and install the equipment. Even more importantly, churches would need to prepare their members and community for this innovative evangelism. Would Brad consider coordinating the preparation work?

Brad had worked extensively with Mark and Ernestine Finley, beginning with the early days of their evangelistic ministry in the eastern United States and extending to our time at the North American Division evangelism institute in Chicago. When Pastor Aufderhar called, we were working for the Adventist Church in central Europe, based in Bern, Switzerland. Brad was conducting church-growth training institutes and evangelistic series across Europe. The NET '95 concept interested us greatly. Our whole ministry has been dedicated to evangelism. The idea that modern satellite technology could spread the spiritual gift of evangelism far beyond one location intrigued us!

The Adventist Church in central Europe graciously agreed to "loan" us back to North America for the project. We prepared materials and began active promotion across the fifty states and Canada.

Early in 1994, Pastor Don and Marjorie Gray stepped in to continue the NET '95 preparation while Brad and I went to Bulgaria to fulfill a prior commitment, a church growth and evangelism institute. Upon our return, the two seasoned evangelists, Pastor Gray and Brad, along with many others, worked together in the final NET '95 preparation at camp meetings and ministerial workers' meetings across the continent.

The biggest challenge NET '95 faced was skepticism concerning the concept of satellite evangelism. The church had never tried anything like this before. Some Adventists believed TV was a tool of the devil. To them and others, the idea of bringing big screen "cinema" into the church seemed sacrilegious. Others did recognize the attractiveness of TV to modern society and thought it could be advantageous. However, evangelism is very personal, and the idea of people coming to watch TV in church and then responding positively to an invitation from a speaker on a screen seemed ridiculous to many.

There were other questions too. Would the corporate church successfully unite in one evangelistic event, with one evangelist, preaching from one host location? Previously, people had conducted evangelistic campaigns involving several churches in a region simultaneously, but never one event involving hundreds of churches. How did satellite NET evangelism differ from regular evangelism, and what plans and materials were necessary for it to succeed? Would the individual churches provide the necessary technology?

The thought that we could oversee the installation of the equipment and training of the personnel and then have churches with widely varying technical resources all successfully use the equipment seemed presumptuous. Could the denomination provide the technical support all these sites would require? The financial resources necessary would also stretch many churches. Would our members provide the support this innovative new project needed?

In personal discussions and one candid administrative meeting after another, leaders confronted the reservations and objections. Many times, the skepticism seemed so thick "you could cut it with a knife." Pastor Al McClure, president of the Adventist Church in North America, and many other leaders gave their strong support and urged the churches to move ahead in faith. Around North America, prayer bands and prayer chains earnestly began to pray for Heaven's blessing and guidance—not only that God would attract spiritual seekers but also that He would bring confirmation and assurance regarding this new method of evangelism.

It would be a miracle if NET '95 were successful. It would take Heaven's intervention to overcome all the reservations and obstacles.

Fishing from the stars

The September 5, 1994, issue of the North Pacific Union Conference *Gleaner* carried an interview that the editor, Ed Schwisow, conducted with Pastor Duane McKey, North Pacific Union Conference ministerial director. The interview, titled "It's Time to Go Fishing From the Stars," described the questions some of the church leaders were wrestling with as they contemplated satellite evangelism. It explained how and why local congregations should "buy in cheap and tie in deep to an efficient, new, tithe-dollar-saving concept to blanket North America with a call to revival and preparation for the Lord's return."

Gleaner: On the surface, Duane, it looks like NET '95 could be a hazardous investment—lots of satellite time, lots of local churches setting up equipment to capture the show—with no guarantee that "video series" are all that effective in church sanctuaries, and leaving, at the end, thousands of dollars of "white elephant" satellite-dish hardware rusting out on church back-forties. Are these risks worth taking?

McKey: Good questions, and ones that many are asking right now on church boards throughout the Northwest. First, let's talk about effectiveness. We know that the large-screen effect of one of our finest evangelists in the world preaching live in a large meeting will be effective. We've tested it—actually, one test was run more than a year ago using a signal being transmitted live of Finley preaching in Russia. After only one meeting, [visitors] were coming forward to the large screen in response to the altar call.

Sure, you can say that Russia was special—that the effect was even more convincing because the signal came from an exotic place. But the sermon—the message—was the same [as what] we're going to be hearing. . . . It is the message that converts. People today believe what they see on a screen—there's no credibility loss, and in other tests run, it's been found that of viewers watching a program on screen and others in the actual hall with the speaker, big-screen viewers are more responsive than their counterparts in the live hall. It's hard to explain, but it's believed that the "large screen effect" of seeing not just a little figure down at the end of a long aisle, but a giant figure, up close—intimately up close—where the personal credibility of the speaker can be scrutinized and every gesture tested for authenticity, accounts for the added response.

Earlier in the summer of 1994, Pastor Don Schneider, president of the Northern California Conference of the Adventist Church, asked for a special broadcast for the Northern California camp meeting. He requested Pastor Al McClure to talk to the camp-meeting audience on Sabbath via satellite from Washington, D.C. (Pastors McClure and Schneider both were members of the committee responsible for developing NET '95.) Pastor McClure was videoed live in Washington, D.C., answering questions that Pastor Don asked him via telephone from the pulpit in Northern California. The people in the audience observed in awe this use of technology. It worked!

To serve the upcoming NET '95 event, the church in North America established Adventist Communication Network (ACN). In spite of all the misgivings and unknowns, the Adventist Church was taking a bold step forward. More and more churches became excited about the concept and began buying and installing equipment in preparation for NET '95.

Next, the church faced a question about the equipment necessary for live satellite production and uplink. Should the church purchase this equipment or rent it? Warren Judd, president of Adventist Media Productions (AMP), and his team decided that the time had come for the church to own its own production and uplink equipment. "It seemed a silly idea to rent uplink trucks for five weeks. It was time to buy our own system," Warren says.

The uplink equipment for NET '95 was brand new. AMP engineer Gerry Betty put together the first flight pack, which was shipped, along with production equipment, to Chattanooga, Tennessee. The stage was set. The time for satellite evangelism had finally come.

Opening night, February 18, 1995

"I could hardly believe what I was seeing," remembers Brad. "I stood at the point between the audience and the backstage [area]. To my right I could see Pastor Finley preaching to the audience of over twenty-five hundred people packed into the auditorium of the Chattanooga Convention

Center. To my left and behind the stage was a TV monitor of the satellite downlink. There was a beautiful, clear picture of Pastor Finley preaching. The signal had traveled 46,500 miles from Chattanooga to the satellite and returned with only a split-second delay. [It was] covering all of North America. Amazing! What a tool with which to share the message of the gospel with millions. In my heart a dream was born that moment of what a blessing this could be to the entire world."

Spiritually informative preaching and excellent music were being beamed every night to 676 Adventist churches across North America, to an estimated audience of sixty-six thousand. Nothing like this had ever happened before in Adventism! Truly, satellite evangelism was a marvel.

At first, Pastor Doug Janssen and the support team fielded hundreds of calls for technical support. But the equipment worked very well. Churches received dependable, clear programs night by night.

God honored the faith and answered the prayers of His people. In Alaska and Hawaii, across Canada and the United States, thousands responded to the advertising and invitations of our members and attended the local Adventist church downlinks. Amazing stories and reports streamed in by fax, phone, and even email, which was very new at that time. In front of large screens in churches, thousands responded to the invitations of Pastor Finley and came forward in commitment.

Believe it or not, satellite evangelism worked!

In an article titled "NET '95 Brings Families Together" published in the *Adventist Review,* Monte Sahlin wrote:

Two years ago when church leaders decided to move ahead and use satellite technology for a massive transcontinental evangelism project, no one knew quite what to expect!

But now they do! Stories upon stories have been emerging about the largest and most-successful evangelistic thrust in the history of the Seventh-day Adventist Church in North America—NET '95.

• Pastor Glenn Woodard in California tells of a traveling businessman who couldn't attend all of the meetings in his hometown, so he found downlink sites in the cities he was going to and attended all the rest!

• A North Carolina congregation decided not to host the series, but on opening night about 25 people literally were knocking on the church's door to attend the series! They had seen some advertisements someplace else and expected this Adventist church to be open. The church, of course, welcomed the people and turned on their machine. . . .

As [Pastor Phil White] visited in the homes of nonmembers who were attending the series, [he] asked for their reactions to the satellite preacher. And their reactions have been "astounding," says White. "People tell me they don't really stop to think about distance. Their comments are all extremely positive."

Overall, there seems to be a major turnaround in attitudes across the division toward the use of satellite technology in the Adventist Church. Kevin James, a pastor in Hattiesburg, Mississippi, described the change best when he said, "Our greatest skeptic has become our strongest advocate."

Perhaps one of the greatest effects of satellite evangelism was its impact on small church congregations. Full-scale evangelism was no longer confined to the large churches that could afford an evangelist and a big series. This new technology made a first-class evangelistic series, with the very best preaching and music, available to all. Everyone everywhere could have access to the same resources. No longer did tiny or remote congregations need to feel inferior or shy about sharing the gospel with their friends and neighbors. They had something exciting and innovative to offer!

Another empowering concept developed as church congregations realized that they were not alone in the struggles of outreach and evangelism. A new, stronger sense of corporate identity swept into the Seventh-day Adventist Church. Members across the continent were joining together for the same event, praying, visiting, giving Bible studies, and making friends for Jesus. This united effort became an energizing and enabling factor in the success of satellite evangelism.

As the church in North America heard the clear, prophetic preaching of Pastor Finley, faith in the unique message of the Bible was reborn. Renewal and revival quietly swept away doubts among members. A confidence was established that would lay the foundation for greater evangelism.

God worked in a remarkable way. Questions were stilled in the minds of thousands of members, pastors, and other leaders who'd had reservations about satellite evangelism. Around the world, Adventist believers heard the reports of NET '95 and marveled.

Most significantly, more than seven thousand new believers were united by baptism with God's family through NET '95.

Section I:
Essential Components

Sacrifice

When the concept of satellite evangelism was proposed, many people said it was too expensive. At that time, video projectors and downlink equipment were significantly more costly than they are today—somewhere between five and seven thousand dollars per church in North America. Small congregations considered this particularly expensive. On top of that, satellite evangelism was an untested concept. So, churches had to exercise a huge amount of sacrificial faith to buy the equipment and prepare to conduct an evangelism event. Astonishingly, several hundred churches took the bold leap of faith, bought the equipment—and discovered that with the blessing of God and proper preparation, satellite NET evangelism really worked!

In third-world countries, the cost of equipping a church seemed preposterous. Was it even right for church leaders to promote a concept that involved such expense? How could the local members afford the equipment? The world Adventist Church provided no subsidies; no big donors were offering financial aid; and on continents like Africa, the regional church organizations couldn't help the local churches purchase satellite downlink equipment. The local church members would have to carry this responsibility themselves.

Pastor Robert Folkenberg, former president of the world Adventist Church, arranged with Pastor Wakaba, president of the Adventist Church in South Africa, to develop the first satellite event for the continent of Africa. It was to take place early in 1998 from Soweto, South Africa. Our family, including our three sons, went to South Africa and stayed for a number of months to coordinate and produce this event.

The church in South Africa caught the vision, but could the rest of this mighty continent catch the same vision? Would the members buy the equipment? No one knew. Some of us believed that when our members understood the possibility, they would want to be included and that, with God's blessing, the technology would be wildly successful. Many were very, very dubious.

At that time in Africa, a downlink equipment package consisting of a 7-foot (2.3-meter) satellite antenna, IRD decoder (receiver), feed horn, and cabling cost approximately fifteen hundred dollars. If a church also purchased a small video projector, the total package cost close to twenty-five hundred dollars. To put this outlay in the perspective of the economy in Africa, the average monthly wage of a laborer then might have been about fifty dollars. In other words, satellite-evangelism equipment cost the local churches more than two or three years' total wages for a member!

Can you imagine how people in first-world countries would have reacted if the church downlink package had cost the equivalent of more than two years of their annual salary? How many churches in North America would have made that kind of investment? Yet in Africa, Eastern Europe, and India our members did just that! Those of us who were leaders in this project were overwhelmed and humbled by stories of the immense financial sacrifice made by church members who wanted to be part of this dynamic new medium of evangelism. We wept and rejoiced in the faith they showed.

The following stories are only a few of the accounts from various areas of the world that illustrate how God miraculously impressed committed Christians to sacrifice. It is no less a miracle for God to move the hearts of His servants to sacrifice their hard-earned resources than to perform other miraculous acts. In establishing the Adventist Television Network, God worked miracles in thousands of situations to provide resources for the churches to buy and install the necessary downlink equipment.

Namibia, February 1998

Early one morning, people in the mission compound awoke to the sounds of the bawling of cows, the bleating of sheep, and the tinkle of goat bells. What was all the noise about? When the Adventist mission president, Pastor L. Mubonenwa, hurried outside, dozens of church members surrounded him. The women had baskets on their heads containing chickens, ducks, and turkeys. The men and boys had brought a herd of livestock to the compound. What was going on?

Weeks before, Pastor Mubonenwa had heard about this new concept called satellite evangelism. (This was the Pentecost '98 program.) Calling the church members together, he explained that by this method, evangelistic meetings being held in Soweto, South Africa, could reach them in the Caprivi region, more than 900 miles (1,500 kilometers) away.

In this isolated strip of land bordering Botswana, Zambia, and Namibia, the people live very simple, seminomadic lives. They are very poor. Often their homes do not have roofs; they're only enclosures of reeds and sticks. Prosperity is measured by the number of animals the people own.

When the church members heard about this special method of evangelism, they wanted to participate even though they didn't understand how it all worked. "How much is it going to cost?" someone asked. The mission president told them, and everyone grew silent. Impossible. Impossible! The members had no money. They had no vehicles to sell or houses to mortgage—no banks from which to obtain a loan. A wave of despair swept through the group. They wanted so badly to share in the satellite NET evangelism from South Africa, but it was impossible. Questions were asked. Gentle complaints were made. There seemed to be no solution.

The sun began to set, and in a land where there is no electricity, the meeting slowly broke up. Our faithful brothers and sisters wandered back to their homes, lit their cooking fires, and sat around them, praying, thinking, and discussing how they could buy the equipment. Finally the answer came. Scattered over the countryside, family after family began to conclude, "We can sell our animals."

Very early the next morning, as dawn began to break over the desert landscape, little groups of people began walking toward the mission. Dividing their flocks and herds, they began bringing their offering to the compound. "Pastor," they said, "we have heard about the evangelism from the sky. We don't have money to buy what is needed. Please take our animals and sell them and buy us this equipment. We don't want to miss out on this new program of our church."

The mission president quizzed them to confirm that they really wanted to sell their animals. In an economy with very little currency exchange, these animals represented the life savings, food, and transportation of our church members.

Jannie Bekker, executive treasurer for the Adventist Church in Southern Africa, recounted the experience to our team, saying the mission had sold the animals in the market, had sent money from the Caprivi region, and now were asking for equipment. There was not a dry eye among us as Jannie explained that this region is a very, very poor part of Africa. If they could participate in satellite evangelism, just about anybody could.

Out under the stars, on the opening night of Pentecost '98, with the help of a small portable generator, the program from Soweto came through clearly. Hundreds of visitors sat on the ground on rocks and crude benches, listening to the powerful preaching of lay evangelist Fitz Henry.

A young pastor of another denomination attended this satellite series. Elias Swartbooi had been sent only a short time earlier to evangelize the Caprivi region. Night by night he listened to evangelist Fitz Henry. As the Bible truths unfolded, he realized he never had understood the Bible so clearly. He continued to study, and eventually, along with many others, was baptized into the Adventist Church.

Pastor Elias is originally from the Damara tribe, who have a distinct language. Seventh-day Adventists have had no presence among this tribe. In fact, the Demara people have experienced very little Christian influence. Pastor Elias wanted to share God's truth with his people, and so he went to Helderberg College in South Africa and studied theology. His family disowned him, and his wife divorced him, but today, Pastor Elias preaches and teaches God's love to his people. He's one of the stars in the Milky Way of God's miracles in satellite evangelism.

By working in the hearts of these dedicated followers of Jesus, the Spirit of God had overcome a seemingly insurmountable problem. The sacrifice of these poor people resulted in many being baptized, among them a pioneering missionary, a modern apostle Paul.

India, February 1998

News of the upcoming NET '98 program came to our leaders in India. Would the church on that subcontinent participate in satellite evangelism?

Church officials shared the information with lay leadership in Mizoram, in northeastern India. This is an area where in recent years the Adventist message has been well received. Our church is growing there and has established many positive contacts in the cities and communities.

In one large church, members held a business meeting to determine how their church would respond to this opportunity. Lengthy discussion ensued, with members rising to give speeches pro and con. After some time it appeared that those who were hesitant would carry the day and the church would bypass the opportunity. Eventually, however, a little woman obviously retired and of advanced years slowly rose to her feet. She had said nothing to this point; but now, with a youthful vigor and vision that seemed to contradict her age, she challenged the congregation, saying that they needed to be more progressive and forward thinking. "This is the way of the future," she said. "We must go in this direction."

Then, matching her vision with her commitment, she pledged from her meager savings a significant amount to help her church buy the equipment. What she pledged was only a widow's mite, but her speech and financial pledge changed the tone of the meeting. The members rallied together, raising the money to order the equipment.

Months later, they had a successful evangelistic experience. They heard the messages of Pastor Dwight Nelson twelve thousand miles away in their mother language of Mizo through the voice of Pastor Colney. They were struck with the wonder of being part of a global church family that was using cutting-edge technology to share the good news of Jesus with their friends and families. This Mizo-land church rejoiced that their elder sister's sacrificial "widow's mite" had changed the day and led them to participate in satellite NET evangelism.

Democratic Republic of Congo, 1999

It was a typical camp meeting in Butembo, North Kivu. Then, on Sunday, during the final meeting, something happened that Pastor Gordon Gray, executive treasurer for the Adventist Church in west-central Africa, will never forget.

The camp meeting was being held outdoors, and the people sat on the ground in front of a simple stage. Colorful umbrellas shielded the six thousand attendees from the hot African sun.

Earlier an announcement had been made that on that Sunday a special offering would be collected for the purchase of satellite equipment. The members were encouraged to consider prayerfully what they could contribute so their churches could participate.

The time came for the offering. The appeal was made. Deacons came forward and placed large containers before the audience. After a prayer, the choir began to sing, and the people started bringing their offerings down the aisles.

In this part of the Democratic Republic of Congo, there is very little currency. So, people often give their tithes and offerings in produce, livestock, and personal possessions. In response to this offering appeal to purchase satellite-evangelism downlink equipment, church members carefully and worshipfully brought everything imaginable. Clothing, lamps, clocks, pictures, dishes, baskets, handicrafts, and fruits and vegetables quickly began to fill the containers. More items were added as the members brought anything they had that the church could sell in the city market. Men pledged to give cows and goats—their livestock. Truckloads of gravel were promised, with the proceeds to be given for evangelism. Some members pledged four or five days of work in trade for money to add to the offering for satellite evangelism.

Pastor Gray couldn't believe his eyes. How could our members give up what little they had?

The singing continued, as did the steady stream of cheerful givers. Toward the end, when nearly everyone had brought something, a little girl came skipping up to the containers. "She must have been only about five years old," Pastor Gray said. "In her hands was a pair of tiny plastic pink thongs—sandals. She carefully deposited her sandals into the overfilled containers and then joyfully skipped barefoot back to her mother. She had given her only pair of shoes. I was overwhelmed with the sacrifice I had just witnessed and realized that indeed the people had given their all, and God would surely bless them for their faith and sacrifice."

About ten thousand dollars was raised in this offering. This was a huge amount for the economy of the area at that time. With the addition of some special subsidies from the regional headquarters, about forty sets of equipment eventually were installed in this country.

Tanzania, June 2001

The church in Tanzania was preparing for the Africa for Christ satellite NET event. Pastor Jere Patzer, president of the Adventist Church in the North Pacific area of the United States, was to be the speaker. Church leaders traveled from one congregation to another, urging members to sacrifice, to do something extraordinary for the success of Africa for Christ. Pastor Steve Bina recalls being quite taken aback by the penetrating question of a church elder asked on Sabbath in front of the entire congregation. "Pastor, what will you give?" the elder queried.

"My wife and I had already prayerfully and sacrificially given all we could," Pastor Bina says. "But looking over the congregation, I realized my answer would have tremendous impact on that church. As I raised a quick prayer to heaven, my mind raced over my possessions. What more could I give? Instantly the answer came. My family had a small audiocassette player for listening to religious music. It was our only source to play recorded music. We particularly enjoyed the music on Sabbath. However, this little 'boom box' was a luxury. Yes, I would sell this and give the money for more satellite equipment."

The downlink in Nhungumalwa, Tanzania

Members in Tanzania sold their animals, bicycles, handicrafts, and even their clothes to buy equipment. In one town, a woman came to our church leaders and said, "I have no bicycle, no animals, no produce, and no clothes to sell. I have only this little chick. Will you accept this gift?"

A chick has no value. It can't be sold for meat. It can't lay eggs. But it was all this woman had—and she gave her all.

As the satellite equipment was purchased and installed, members from other denominations came to the Adventist members, inquiring, "You are as poor as we are; how in the world can you own all this expensive technology?" Many of these querying folk came to the same local Adventist churches to enjoy the satellite programs. Because the interest was so great, often the churches would be completely empty. The equipment was set up outside the churches, with hundreds and sometimes even thousands watching on large screens whitewashed onto the side of the church or from multiple TV sets.

In less than six months, the downlink network in Tanzania grew from 99 sites to 220. This represents an investment of nearly three hundred thousand dollars—amazing, considering that these people received no outside financial support and lived in a country where unemployment is high. What a powerful witness to faithfulness, dedication, and sacrifice! The Adventist church in Tanzania reported nearly thirty-four thousand baptisms from this satellite event. Surely, God honored the faith and sacrifice of those who gave so much.

Romania, February 2002

In an email dated February 22, 2002, Pastor Adrian Bocaneanu shared this story: In a rural area in the Oltenia region of Romania, a group of Adventist believers started a new church building. When it was almost finished, the youngest and ablest members of the congregation left to find work elsewhere. The remaining members found it very difficult to complete the church, which was by now too large for the size of the congregation. They began discussing what they were going to do.

The answer to their predicament? Evangelism! Evangelism would fill their empty church.

Soon, Pastor Lucian Cristescu, executive secretary of the Adventist Church in Romania, would be the speaker for The Galilean. It was going to be the first NET evangelism event with a Romanian speaker, and the members of the church in Oltenia didn't want to miss it. They decided to take an offering so they could buy the satellite equipment package, which would cost them approximately twelve hundred dollars.

The pastor officiated as the members of the congregation made commitments. "I give 500,000 lei," someone said. This amounts to approximately fifteen dollars. It's about what an elderly person receives as a monthly pension.

"I give one million lei."

"I'll give the hundred dollars that my son sent me from Spain."

And so the pledges were made. When the amount pledged totaled a little less than two-thirds of what was needed, it seemed that those present had given all they could. A long silence followed, and the members began to think that they would have to abandon their dreams of having the equipment to participate in the satellite NET series. Then a very old man, his back bent by hard work on the farms, calmly said, "I give one million lei."

The pastor couldn't believe his ears. He knew this man was really poor. Finally, he asked him, "Are you sure you want to pledge that amount? Where can you get this money?"

Quietly, the man answered, "This is the money I have saved for my funeral. Who knows what the plans of the Lord are?"

To understand the significance of this gift, one must know the culture of Romania. There, people save money for their funeral. It is considered a sacred obligation. It wouldn't be right to burden the family members left behind with one's funeral expenses.

This pledge electrified the church. This old man would give his funeral money? Satellite evangelism was so important that he would risk complete poverty and dishonor to support the project? A new round of commitments started, and in a few minutes, the pastor had to close the pledges as they had more commitments than needed to buy all the equipment.

Today, the Adventist Television Network links more than twenty thousand churches worldwide. This represents a tremendous investment. Behind every downlink site, there is a miracle of the Holy Spirit impressing hearts to empty pocketbooks to provide these broadcasts to friends and neighbors. Space doesn't permit us to tell more of these miracles. However, more than money, this network represents an incredible spirit of faith and sacrifice. Members brought their "loaves and fishes"—what was in their hands—and God multiplied these humble gifts to bless millions. It's not the equipment that has made satellite NET evangelism and the Hope Channels a success. It's the dedication and sacrifice of individuals who willingly give their all to advance God's work.

Installation

"Now that we have paid this money, how do we get all this equipment to work?" We heard this question many times as we prepared for satellite NET evangelism events. Usually, professionals install the satellite reception equipment. But in many areas of the world, either because of finances or because no installers were available, church members had to install this equipment themselves.

The satellites are approximately 23,500 miles up in space and orbit over the equator in a very small circle. To receive the signal, the dish antenna must be stable and pointed ("tuned") accurately. The LNB, the device in front of the dish, must be rotated into the correct position. The cabling must be connected with no kinks or breaks, and it mustn't be too long. The receiver must be properly programmed with a number of parameters and settings. The video projector must be appropriately connected. And all of this equipment is relatively delicate and must be handled carefully and connected to a stable power source.

Each of these steps presents opportunity for error and for the evil one to interfere. Make just one incorrect setting, and the entire installation won't work. And of course, the closer the start date of a satellite NET event looms, the greater the pressure becomes. Nobody wants something to go wrong during a broadcast when a large audience is present! The success of the worldwide Adventist Television Network hinges on thousands of dedicated local church technicians who faithfully learn to operate this technology.

In first-world countries, which tend to have more of a technical orientation, the above complexities are difficult enough. But in third-world countries, where there is generally little technical awareness, the task of correctly installing the equipment is monumentally difficult. Sometimes members in these areas had never previously used a telephone or held a television remote control. Installing and operating the equipment was very foreign and intimidating. How on earth could they be expected to manage the satellite downlink equipment?

Often, well-intentioned but misguided efforts and/or the machinations of the evil one necessitated God's miraculous intervention for His people to make and maintain a proper satellite downlink installation. Added to this, in some areas the local security situation of our churches necessitates that the projection and receiver equipment, including the LNB on the dish, be removed after every program and reinstalled before the next. Each such operation poses the danger of damaging the equipment or making an incorrect installation.

In some areas of the world, church leaders developed technical support centers that people could telephone, fax, or email for assistance. However, in large parts of the world, the available communication infrastructure is too limited, fragile, or expensive for our members to use. So the correct installation and operation of the equipment depended entirely on pre-event training and the ingenuity of the local technicians entrusted with the responsibility. Many said that satellite evangelism would fail because of this factor.

The ATN staff developed training manuals, training seminars, videos, and Internet sites to provide technical support for the world network. Although we've done our best, often this was not enough. We've seen God work in remarkable ways to overcome local limitations.

When you consider all these factors, you have to conclude it's a miracle that the Adventist Television Network exists and that these satellite NET events have experienced the success they have. The following stories are but a very brief sampling of the providential experiences with which God has blessed the church, as our world family has ventured into satellite NET evangelism.

United States, October 1996

In an article in the November 1996 Lake Union Conference *Herald,* Pastor Franklyn Horne told of a miracle:

A satellite reception system had been donated to the Cadillac church. Nobody realized that the satellite-dish positioning motor was not functioning so the dish could not be turned toward the proper satellite. After hours of working on it, the crew prayed, "Lord, we need Your help." Pastor Franklyn Horne and one of the members climbed up on the roof to aim the dish manually, knowing the odds of doing so successfully were near nil. Again they prayed, "Lord, it's up to You." They turned the dish a quarter turn, then climbed down and went back inside. When they turned the system back on, the signal came in perfectly.

The next week Pastor Horne went and bought a new motor. They installed it and began trying to tune in to the satellite. At 6:50 Tuesday night, they had still not been successful. So they pulled the new motor off and installed the old one that hadn't worked. Again they prayed, "Lord, this is Your program. You're going to have to do this. We can't." When they turned the system on again, the signal came in perfectly.

From a human perspective, this story is absurd. People don't just hook up their equipment, randomly point their dish at the sky, and expect it to work. But the story's true! Obviously, God did something special for this church. Similar experiences happened around the world many times.

Germany, NET '98

"Dieses Problem ist unlösbar!" ("There's no solution to this problem!") Close to the Adventist church in Goettingen stood three large, healthy oak trees. One of them blocked the line of sight between the church and the satellite. The trees were more than one hundred years old and were protected by German law. The municipality "forbids the removal or tampering of heritage property. You may not cut the trees or trim them."

When the official word came back to the members of Goettingen church, they were sad. They had purchased the satellite equipment and were busy preparing for NET '98. But the installer informed them there was no way to receive the satellite signal because one of the trees was blocking the signal. It seemed their participation in satellite NET evangelism was doomed.

Was there any way out of this difficulty, which, from a human perspective, seemed impossible to overcome? It seemed their only hope was a miracle, but what would it be? No one had any idea.

God works in mysterious ways. During the final week before the start of the satellite-evangelism program, a huge storm developed. Rain poured down, the wind blew fiercely, and several bolts of lightning struck the center of the city. One of them split one of the trees in front of the church—the tree that was blocking the satellite signal. Almost before the members knew what had happened, city workers were on site with chainsaws, cutting down what remained of that tree. By the end of the day it was gone, and the satellite installer had a clear signal coming into the church!

Ghana, March 1999

"Dad, I think I can tune the dishes. I've been watching Ian Miller and Pastor François Louw. They even let me try with their compasses, and I got the signal. Why don't you let me go and help the churches—there are so many to do?"

Eleven-year-old Chris Thorp was eager to assist in the preparation for ACTS 2000—Ghana. Brad thought a moment and said, "Well, Son, if you think you can really do it on your own, we can send you with some of the elders who come every day asking for help."

Soon the perfect opportunity presented itself. A couple churches on the outskirts of Kumasi needed help, and the elders came asking for a technician. Brad said to them, "Take my son. He'll help you."

The elders were silent for a moment. They looked at the young boy. How could this slender lad tune the dishes? The problem was that no one else was available to go. Many churches needed assistance, and there weren't enough experienced technicians to help them all. So, despite their uncertainty, the elders agreed to give Chris a try.

Handing Chris a compass and some other necessary tools and equipment, we wished him good luck. With a prayer and an admonition to the elders to care for him and his safety, we watched Chris leave. Would he really be able to tune the dish correctly?

When Chris got to the church, the other church members were even more dubious. If they couldn't find the satellite, how could this young kid do it?

With a quiet smile and a prayer in his heart, Chris climbed up the tower to adjust the LNB. Then, consulting the compass, he began to move the dish slowly until he thought it was pointing in the right direction. After adjusting the elevation to the correct angle, he climbed down and began to work with the receiver, correctly entering all the parameters. Within less than ten minutes, the picture and sound came in loud and clear.

A joyous cheer rose from all the anxious spectators standing around. The elders who had brought Chris breathed a huge sigh of relief. Apparently, this kid really did know something.

On the following days, Chris kept a compass hung around his neck. And whenever requests for help came that the other technicians couldn't fill, he was prepared to go. Soon word got around, and people came to the office asking for "the young boy" to help them.

One day, Brad had the chance to go along with Chris and watch him tune a church downlink dish. When they got to the location, Brad's heart went into his throat, and a chill ran up his back. The satellite dish was attached to a pillar nearly forty-five feet (fifteen meters) high. Positioned close beside it was a partial platform supported by a skimpy, unsteady scaffolding made of thin tree trunks with branches for steps spaced about two feet apart.

"Chris, you can't go up on that!"

A church in Kumasi, Ghana, with the downlink that Chris tuned

"Oh, Dad, this is nothing. This is what I've been climbing almost everywhere. Don't worry about me; I can do this," Chris said with a laugh as he started to climb the scaffold. He thought it was funny to see his dad so unnerved! A short discussion followed in which Brad firmly told the local church leaders that their setup was too unsafe and that only after they lowered their pole and dish would he allow Chris to come back and tune their equipment.

When Brad inquired of the church members why they had put the satellite dish so high, they responded by saying that they had been told to put it as high as possible so that thieves wouldn't bother the equipment. Brad groaned. He had instructed that the dishes should be positioned high enough to deter vandalism and to give an unobstructed view of the satellite. The Ghanaian members had taken the instructions seriously; all across the country they had painstakingly erected tall, slender concrete pillars to protect the precious satellite equipment. But Brad hadn't imagined that his advice would be taken to this height!

In a short time, 112 churches all across Ghana were equipped for this event, and no one was injured in all these difficult installations. Some of the thousands of downlink sites around the world are in very precarious situations. As far as we know, no one has suffered serious harm while installing the satellite equipment. We thank God for His protection and mercy.

Ghana, March 1999

Knock, knock, knock came the gentle tapping on the production house door in Kumasi, Ghana. Going to the door, Brad welcomed a timid young man who was carefully holding a paper package with a receiver.

"How can I help you?" asked Brad.

Very slowly, with limited English, the young man explained that he couldn't get the IRD (receiver) to work. Was the IRD broken? Would Pastor Brad please help him?

We had faced this situation scores of times. How were we to teach people who had no technical background to install and run their equipment? We had tried numerous ways. We had held seminars and prepared manuals, but somehow they seemed too complicated for many people.

A few days earlier, remembering a series of books titled *Computers for Dummies* that were available in North America, I had laughingly said to my boys, "We need to prepare an instruction sheet that even I can understand!" I'm not a "techie" person. I have trouble putting a key in a lock. I've always left technical matters to the professional technicians on our staff. I had suggested that they should prepare a simple instruction sheet. But so many people needed help, and there seemed to be no time for preparing a simplified guide. How could a technical dummy like me help these people?

Taking a sheet of paper, I plugged in a receiver and started from the very beginning. Simplifying the instructions that had been prepared, I wrote:

Step one: Push "Menu" button.
Step two: Push the down arrow button three times to select "Receiver set up."
Step three: Push "Select" . . .

And on I wrote. I was a "dummy," and I needed to figure out how to make this thing work so I too could help others. Within an hour, I had completed a one-page, simple, step-by-step instruction summary. It worked. I could get the signal on my own.

Brad invited the young man to a table, and he carefully took out the receiver. Connecting the cables, Brad determined that it was functioning properly.

"Can you read these instructions?" Brad asked, referring to the sheet I had written.

The young man, whose mother language was Twi, nodded yes.

"This is the remote control. Do you understand what these words on the buttons mean?" Brad asked.

"Yes," came the nervous and hesitant answer.

"All right, take the remote control, read the instructions, and do exactly what each step tells you to do. Take your time," said Brad.

With hands shaking in nervousness, the young man took the remote control and focused on the simplified instruction sheet. Slowly, one by one, he followed each step. Suddenly his face broke out in a huge smile. He had the picture. He'd done it—it worked!

After several reviews, the young man was on his way, and another church was receiving the nightly programs.

It Is Written reported forty thousand baptisms from the ACTS 2000—Ghana event.

Ukraine, September 1999

"Brad, I have no idea why I can't get reception. I've repositioned the dish. I've tried several different LNBs. I've spent hours with the equipment, and I can't bring in a signal. Nothing!"

Ian Miller scratched his head and continued. "I don't know what else to try. I've exhausted all possibilities. With the dish sited up on the roof, there seems to be no reason why we shouldn't be getting a good signal."

Ian and Brad were at the church headquarters in Kiev, Ukraine. Ian is a retired radio and TV engineer. He and his wife, Velma, volunteer their service for ATN. They've given thousands of hours and traveled hundreds of thousands of miles installing equipment and training church technicians. Ian had worked for more than forty years in the broadcast industry in a very wide variety of situations; he is very experienced with antenna installations. But this installation in Kiev had him stumped! He had spent nearly two whole days working on it and still couldn't get a signal. What on earth was the problem?

Brad joined him on the roof. He mused to himself that if Ian couldn't get a signal, no one could. Again they went through all the steps. There still was no signal. They discussed every possible factor they could think of. There shouldn't be a technical problem—it must be something else.

Ian thought it might be microwave interference. Others suggested that cold war radio-jamming equipment might be the problem. Still others suggested conspiracy theories. Ian consulted with a local broadcast engineer. He couldn't offer any solutions. Never in all of Ian's years of experience had he come up short like this. He was baffled and frustrated!

Brad, Ian, and the other workers bowed their heads and prayed. "Lord, this is Your work; please show us what to do. Help us to find a solution!"

Then, carefully, they began looking around the vicinity again. They saw nothing that could be causing the problem. Standing there puzzled and nearly ready to give up, Ian decided to move the dish to a wall about twelve feet (four meters) from where it had been. Immediately, he got a signal with exceptional quality and strength. What had happened? What had been the problem?

Believe it or not, a doghouse had caused the trouble! For security purposes, several guard dogs were released on the Adventist Church headquarters compound each night. During the day, these dogs were kept in a strong doghouse that stood in front of the dish installation. Every time Ian had climbed to the roof, these dogs had very vocally let him know he didn't belong there.

Now Ian realized that the roof on the doghouse just happened to be at the correct angle to reflect the satellite signal into the antenna dish and cancel the signal coming to the dish directly from the satellite. The new location had eliminated the interference from the doghouse, allowing for clear reception.

Zambia, August 2003

"Something great is happening here!" enthusiastically reported Pastor Mulambo, ATN satellite coordinator for the Adventist Church in Zambia. It was August 29, 2003—the opening night of the Hope for a Troubled World satellite NET evangelism program with Pastor Lonnie Melashenko, uplinked from Lusaka, Zambia. Yes, something great really was happening, but first the leaders and members of the Adventist Church in Zambia had to go through a Red Sea experience.

For nearly two years, church leaders there had dreamed of having five hundred churches participating in a NET evangelism series. More than 150 sites were already equipped. Now, the members pooled together their resources, and the Voice of Prophecy added a subsidy. Months before the meetings were to open, three hundred churches put in their orders for the necessary equipment.

The order for the necessary equipment was placed with a supplier outside of Zambia. Patiently the churches waited for the delivery. Eventually, the

IRDs (receivers) came, but no satellite dishes and no LNBs. The weeks ticked by with no sign of these necessary items.

After intense investigation, Pastor Musonda, executive treasurer for the Adventist Church in Zambia, discovered that the company selling the satellite equipment had not acted honestly. Instead of shipping the equipment by air from Asia as promised, they had shipped it via an ocean liner. There was no possibility of it arriving in time for the satellite event. The devil was indeed busy making mischief to disrupt this series!

What were those planning the meetings to do? The success of the series was in jeopardy unless other equipment could be found and installed, but the meetings were due to start in less than three weeks. The company might eventually refund the money. However, the churches had worked long and hard to get the initial funds. They couldn't raise more money. So, unless a way could be found to supply the equipment, there would be huge disappointment. But finding that much equipment in Africa and at a reasonable cost would be no easy feat!

The Lusaka dish-manufacturing team

Emails and phone calls crisscrossed the ocean. And the ATN leaders and Zambian church leaders implored Heaven's intervention as they sought to accomplish the impossible.

How did God provide an answer?

The few satellite dishes available locally were purchased. Someone found and bought additional dishes in South Africa, along with three hundred LNBs. And ATN sponsored Enoch Mogusu, a resourceful lay leader from Kenya, to come to Lusaka and bring some of his homemade dish manufacturing equipment. With Enoch's instruction, lay members worked around the clock to manufacture dishes from locally sourced materials. Ultimately, this lay team constructed more than sixty 7-foot (2.3-meter) satellite dishes that were put into immediate use.

Reminiscing, Errol Van Eck, ATN technical information coordinator, says,

> I believe it was providential that [twelve days before the beginning of the event] our leaders found a layman in Lusaka who had a metal workshop available, which he immediately offered for the dish-making operation. He had the tools we needed and particularly a compressor for the spray-painting, which would have been expensive to hire. In many other ways he helped us and showed an interest in what we were doing.
>
> The day before traveling to Lusaka, I went to the nearest hardware store and bought sixteen high-speed, titanium-tipped drill bits. I had no idea why. Later, I learned that the square tube available in Zambia was much heavier and difficult to drill. . . . The titanium bits turned out to be invaluable and stayed sharp for much longer than those available locally, helping to keep the operation going.

Eight days before the start of the program, by faith, Pastor Musonda and Dr. Chikwekwe boarded the plane in South Africa with sixty LNBs that the church had no possibility of preclearing through customs. They had no money to pay the expected high customs charges. After fervent prayer, at the last possible moment, the Lord provided. Customs cleared all of the equipment with no charges!

On the same day, a truck burdened with the weight of 120 satellite dishes and 240 LNBs left Johannesburg, South Africa, bound for Lusaka. Because of the condition of the roads and the excess weight, the driver had to repair seven flat tires along the way!

Enoch Mogusu's satellite dishes

When the shipment finally arrived at the border between Zimbabwe and Zambia, the truck and all the goods were impounded because something was missing in the paperwork. (It seemed the devil tried everything!) At the cost of another day, the missing paper was faxed and the load cleared. The truck ground into Lusaka only two days before the start of the satellite series.

Church members from all over Zambia were camping in the yard of the church headquarters, waiting for the equipment. You can imagine their eagerness as they carried the dishes hundreds of kilometers back to their churches with only hours to go before the meetings started.

Dr. Chikwekwe reported,

Technicians worked day and night—literally! And in five days, all 114 downlinks in the city of Lusaka are up and running, with one site reporting a viewing audience of three thousand! We believe 85 percent of all the 450 plus sites in Zambia are up and running. There are a few rural locations we are not sure about because communication is quite difficult. But we have seen miracle after miracle—it is truly amazing what God has done! (Reported in *ATN NewsNotes #* 19, September 4, 2003.)

What the Lord helped our church in Zambia to accomplish in eighteen days was truly extraordinary! In the city of Lusaka, with a population of 1.2 million, 114 downlinks are now united in sharing the gospel. Each one stands as a testimony of triumph against the adversary, who tried hard to stop the Hope for a Troubled World series across Zambia. In 2004, Zambia reported more than 750 churches equipped and part of the Adventist Television Network.

ATN has seen many other occasions—although possibly not as dramatic as this one—when God has helped churches and other organizations find equipment. The books of heaven will reveal the many sincere prayers that ascended there from faithful members as they struggled to find, install, and operate the equipment for satellite NET evangelism.

Equipment

Satellite evangelism depends on a complex technical system that is very fragile and subject to many problems. A broken wire, a blown fuse, a transistor that doesn't work, an overloaded electrical circuit, a faulty machine—all can wreak havoc. The ATN team worked valiantly to avoid problems, yet many times they witnessed God's intervention in the midst of technical difficulties that occurred despite their best efforts.

To facilitate the multilanguage broadcast for the Adventist Church, ATN had special encoding equipment custom built and packaged in "flyaway" cases for transportation. A generous donation from the Chan Shun Foundation financed this encoder. Our twenty-channel encoder is unique to the broadcast industry. Not even the large networks like CNN, NBC, and BBC have encoders with this capacity.

The production and broadcasting of each satellite NET evangelism program requires on location nearly five tons of technical gear: uplink equipment, the encoder, production equipment, and public address and audio sound systems. Often a portable power generator is also needed. Though we maintain this equipment carefully, sometimes things go wrong. These tense situations raise a call for prayer as our technical staff, often under a lot of pressure, struggles to find solutions.

The Adventist Media Production (AMP) team led by Warren Judd provides most of the technical services for the Adventist Television Network. This team is phenomenal! Hundreds of times, they have disassembled, packed, shipped, assembled, maintained, and done a thousand other things to assure quality production and broadcast. They have traveled extensively, leaving their families and adapting to scores of cultural environments in order to spread the gospel. Considering the potential for error, very little has gone wrong. When trouble has arisen, the team members have been innovative and persistent at providing solutions. It is hard to imagine what the Adventist Television Network and the Hope channels would be without the dedicated work of AMP.

Mobile production room with director Colin Mead and engineer Gerry Betty

Africa, May 1998

In Lusaka, Zambia, more than three thousand people eagerly packed into the courtyard of one of our churches nightly to hear and see the messages relayed by satellite. One night, just before the program was to begin, the public address system amplifier emitted a loud bang followed by a stream of smoke, and then it stopped working. For the large crowd to hear the message, that amplifier had to work. No other amplifier was available on short notice.

The church elders and deacons gathered around the faulty equipment, prayed, and then switched the amplifier back on. After a few crackles, it boomed out—just as the images appeared on the screens. The audience heard the sound clearly all evening.

After the service, the deacon responsible for the sound system carefully removed the back of the amplifier. He found nothing inside except a pile of charred wires and ashes. Yet this burned-out amplifier had worked for two hours!

United States, October 1998

NET '98 was a major undertaking for the Adventist Church and particularly for the technical staff. It was the first satellite NET evangelism series that was to be transmitted in forty languages for full, worldwide participation. Each program was to be broadcast four times from Andrews University to accommodate audiences in different time zones around the world. Nearly five thousand Adventist churches worldwide would join in this event.

Satellite uplink trucks lined the sidewalks of Pioneer Memorial Church. Downstairs, the fellowship hall was transformed as carpenters erected forty booths for the translators coming from around the globe. Then, in the final hours before the first broadcast, serious problems challenged us.

"Brad," Warren Judd said, "something's wrong with the uplink. I have no idea what the problem is, what the solution is, who can help us, or, if we need parts, how to get them here in time. But unless we fix this problem, there won't be any broadcast!" Warren and his team were preoccupied with other troubles that had arisen at the last minute and didn't have the time or the personnel to deal with the encoder problem that had developed.

This was a disaster!

We bowed our heads and laid the problem out before the Lord of the universe. Drs. John and Millie Youngberg led the prayer ministry at Pioneer Memorial Church. Throughout the day, prayer groups gathered on campus, and in emergencies like this, they alerted prayer chains across North America, who petitioned God's intervention.

Brad called the engineering department of the company in Atlanta that had manufactured the encoder. We had paid a lot of money for this specialized equipment, and it wasn't doing everything it was supposed to. However, it didn't seem help was forthcoming, and the deadline loomed over our team.

Eventually, Brad reached the vice president of the company that manufactured the encoder and explained our difficulty. We had to find the right person to help us immediately. Within hours, an engineer was on a plane from Atlanta, tasked to stay with our team until the encoder and uplink were fully functioning.

The engineer arrived, and in a relatively short time fixed the encoder. However, the uplink for the Pacific Rim was still not functioning. The churches in Australia and around the Pacific Ocean could not receive the test broadcasts. A solution had to be found. Finally, the problem was identified in the uplink truck, parts were ordered, and just hours before the program began, we had successful test broadcasts.

In retrospect, it might seem that the problems were simply matters of engineering. But in the final hours of preparation for this major, first-time event, the pressure on the technical and coordination team was immense. We had relatively little experience, and we had to make this work! There was no room for error. God helped us in this extremity with special wisdom and providences to find solutions.

NET '98 resulted in more than twenty-five thousand baptisms around the globe. The confidence it built also laid the foundation for the world network that exists today.

England, October 1998

Pastor Dalbert Elias, NET '98 coordinator for the Adventist Church in the United Kingdom, sent the following email:

> It was the second night of NET '98 with Pastor Dwight Nelson. The Leeds Adventist church (North England) had newly installed equipment. They had been having problems much of the afternoon with the audio. Minutes before the visitors arrived, the picture also failed.
>
> Having checked everything—cables, connections—and also having unplugged and replugged into the power source, they still had no reception. Clearly, the IRD wasn't going to work. What were they going to do? How could they disappoint their members and visitors?
>
> Pastor Des Rafferty called fifteen members to join him in prayer around the malfunctioning receiver. He and his operator laid their hands on the receiver, and all earnestly prayed. The group was impressed to switch everything off and back on again.
>
> Wonderfully, the faulty receiver they had been struggling with came alive: Picture, sound, everything was there! Night two of NET '98 was up and running, thanks to answered prayer.

Clearly, God was backing NET '98.

Romania, September 1999

"Brad, if the uplink dish isn't on a flight out of Miami within three hours, there will be no satellite evangelism Friday night."

Brad had just arrived in Romania for the NET 2000 series with Pastor Mark Finley. The production team, aided by Denzil and Donna McNeilus, had been busy setting up their equipment at the Great Hall of the Palace. Vital to the series was the uplink dish that sends the signal to the satellite. Adventist Media Productions had purchased a new uplink dish, and it was supposed to have been sent days before, but it hadn't come. Now, the reality was that unless someone caught an airline flight to Romania and brought the dish as part of their baggage, it wouldn't arrive on time.

What to do? Pray. This was a major crisis. Without the uplink dish, there would be no satellite broadcast.

While the team prayed, Brad went to the closest phone. Could they get a ticket on such short notice? Who had a passport? Calling a good friend, Pastor Ralph Ringer, in the Florida Conference office, Brad explained the urgent problem.

"Well," Ralph said, "we have a secretary, Adriana Pasos, who is originally from Romania. Maybe she can help."

"Does she have a valid passport?" queried Brad.

Minutes ticked by.

"Yes, she does," came the answer from Ralph.

"Would she be willing to travel immediately to Romania if we can get her a ticket?" asked Brad.

"Yes. But remember she's here in Orlando, and the flight leaves from Miami." (Orlando is approximately 225 miles [350 km] from Miami.)

"Well, let me see if we can get a ticket for her," answered Brad.

To complicate matters, someone had to arrange for the dish manufacturer to deliver the dish and all the boxes that went with it to the passenger ticket counter in Miami. One phone wasn't enough to handle this crisis. Brad was in Bucharest. He called me in British Columbia and rapidly explained the situation. "Find the next flight out of Miami and book it," he said. "By God's grace, Adriana will make it. Do everything possible to get her on that flight. I'll work with the manufacturer to get the dish to the counter at the same time."

Moments later, I told Brad, "I have a ticket," and Brad told me, "They'll deliver the dish if she gets there on time."

A frantic phone call to Ralph Ringer followed. "Ralph, can Adriana catch a flight to Miami?"

"Yes, but she needs a ticket and money and some clothes. She has two small children and a home to care for."

Brad replied, "Ralph, this is an emergency. If we don't get her to Miami in ninety minutes, this satellite evangelism series won't launch. Can the Florida Conference advance the money for tickets and travel?"

So began a high-speed drama. Obtaining some travel money from the treasurer of the Florida Conference, Ralph quickly drove Adriana to her home, where she had time only to grab her American passport. On the way to the airport, she phoned her husband and explained the situation. (Thank God for supportive understanding husbands!) Could they reach the Orlando airport in time to catch the next commuter flight to

Miami? Would seats be available? Would there be enough time to buy a ticket?

Meanwhile, back in British Columbia, I secured a ticket from Lufthansa airlines for Adriana's flight from Miami to Romania. Then I sat at my desk and prayed. While I was praying, I felt impressed to call the Miami airport and ask to speak to a Lufthansa supervisor to alert people there about this special situation. The connection was very tight; Adriana would arrive from Orlando less than forty-five minutes before the international flight to Europe. She would have to connect with the person who was bringing the equipment and then check in.

A few phone calls later, I had managed to reach the right department in Miami International Airport. A man with a German accent answered my call. I asked to speak to the supervisor on duty. He answered that he was the manager for Lufthansa Miami. Perfect! I told him about our event in Bucharest and that the equipment must leave on this flight. He listened carefully, asked some questions, and then agreed to go personally to the counter and see that Adriana and the baggage got on the flight.

Meanwhile, in Romania, Donna and Denzil McNeilus and the team continued praying. Brad was on the phone with the dish manufacturer and his freight agent in Miami. Yes, they would deliver, but they had to meet Adriana at a specified time; they couldn't wait in the airport for her.

Back in Orlando, Ralph and Adriana arrived at the airport. A seat was available for the flight to Miami. They got a ticket, and she was on her way with only the clothes she was wearing, a passport, and a few dollars, leaving behind a puzzled family.

The Delta flight from Orlando to Miami arrived slightly late. Once out of the plane, Adriana ran as fast as she could to the international departures terminal, but now the time for the delivery of the dish had passed. In Romania, Brad was on the phone to the freight agent. In Canada, I was on the phone to the Lufthansa counter.

Breathless, Adriana got to the counter. Yes, the freight forwarder would come back and deliver. Five minutes before departure, clutching ticket and precious baggage tags, Adriana was the last passenger to board the flight for Europe. Three-and-a-half hours after the drama started, miraculously, Adriana was winging her way over the Atlantic, shepherding the precious dish for the ACTS 2000 Bucharest series. God answered prayers and performed miracles.

Arriving safely and clearing customs, Adriana was met with a royal welcome! Quickly, the team went to work to assemble the uplink dish. Time raced by, and, miraculously again, the uplink was tested and operative five minutes before the broadcast began!

The following week I called the Lufthansa office in Miami, hoping to thank the manager for his assistance. I called on four different occasions and never was able to reach him. This increased my belief that the Lord helped us by having him available when we needed him most.

It Is Written and the Adventist Church in Romania reported more than twenty-two thousand baptisms from ACTS 2000—Romania.

Australia, 2001

"I can't believe it! This deal is just too good to be true! If we can purchase the van for less than 25 percent of its original cost, that will be a miracle!" David Gibbons was excited. This van would solve some major problems for the Adventist Media Centre in Sydney.

After NET '98, the South Pacific region of the world church wanted to develop their own mobile media ministry. The church has an excellent TV studio in Sydney. However, to serve the needs of their constituency, they needed some way of doing mobile production.

David looked longingly at the commercial TV production trucks often used by the big networks. This could never be an option. It would be much too expensive for their budget.

The technical staff prayed that the Lord would provide an answer to their need. Then David learned that the New South Wales Technical and Further Education (TAFE) organization had a production van they no longer needed. It was fully equipped—a complete television control room on wheels. And they would sell it to us for less than 25 percent of what it had cost to set it up. Gratefully, the Adventist Media Centre purchased the van.

David Gibbons, AMC marketing director, reported in the South Pacific Division *Record:*

The van arrived just in time to be used in Mark Finley's Papua New Guinea campaign in July 2001. Adventist Media took a full dubbing suite to Port Moresby during the Mark Finley campaign and sold over nine thousand videos during the sixteen-night program, which saw crowds of over one hundred thousand every night at the host site. A local major TV network took the Adventist Media production the following day and broadcast the program again to an anticipated audience of one million people nationally.

What a gift from God it was. Since that time, it has been used with various programs, including the Philip Yancey satellite uplink, and *The Essential Jesus* book launch. In the Rez 10 satellite evangelism project, the truck toured Adelaide, Melbourne, Canberra, Sydney, and Brisbane

David Gibbons and the mobile uplink van in Australia

over ten days to record and uplink the successful youth "underground" program. To hire a similar truck for [only] these programs would have cost us in excess of $100,000. But we were able to purchase this amazing asset for less than $80,000. Now it can be used for other ventures the church has in mind.

As confidence in satellite NET evangelism has grown, different entities of the world church have begun to invest to provide greater production capacity. This has not happened quickly. In 1995, the church operated only two media centers. As of 2004, the ATN world church network comprises forty media centers of varying size. And on every continent but Antartica, God has opened the doors and helped the church make very economical investments.

Success in Africa

Numerous reports have come to us with amazing stories of the evangelistic success satellite technology has brought throughout Africa. People walked hours through the mountains of Tanzania to a village where a downlink had been set up. In Rwanda, crowds swelled to more than fifteen thousand at the Remero Adventist Church in Kigali. In some remote villages in Ghana, all the inhabitants came to the meetings. In Nigeria, people climbed trees in the overfilled courtyards of churches to watch the programs.

Many, many locations had no electricity, and the entire downlink and public address systems were run on small generators. At night in the villages where there was no electricity, the Adventist church and the satellite program

Uplink gear on location in Kumasi, Ghana

provided excellent "entertainment." Plywood sheets painted white, whitewashed walls, or white fabric panels stitched together and stretched across the side of the church or between trees served as screens. In Dar es Salaam, members brought their TVs to church and set them up throughout the crowds, which sometimes numbered between three thousand and five thousand.

ATN leadership were confronted with the reality that the cost of equipment, limited availability, and the challenge of training members to install and tune the equipment significantly restricted growth. We sent staff from North America and Europe to provide training. These training sessions were effective, but nothing seemed to catch the imagination at the grassroots level. We needed something special to happen. We needed a miracle to bridge the difficult logistical and technical gap and bring ownership of satellite evangelism by the African people.

As a partial solution to the problem, ATN conducted a training seminar in connection with the Christ 2001 satellite NET series in Mwanza, Tanzania. In partnership with local fields, we invited church technicians to attend and learn how to install and maintain the downlink equipment. All the while we prayed that God would help us find a way to put this technology into the hands of our members and inspire broad-based local ownership of satellite evangelism.

God answered this need and our prayers in a remarkable way. He sent Enoch Mogusu, a dedicated lay leader, to the Mwanza training event. Enoch is passionate about evangelism and gifted with innovative technical ideas. Miraculously, God provided the answer for our problem in Africa through this humble tradesman.

Nothing is impossible with God, and our African brothers and sisters proved this as they embraced satellite evangelism with sacrifice, ingenuity, and prayer.

Kenya, 2001

"Dear God, our people love satellite evangelism but have difficulty purchasing satellite dishes. They are so expensive. I wonder if the antennas could be built from materials we have available locally?" prayed Enoch Mogusu in his workshop in Kiisi, Kenya. Enoch had established a small business as a metal fabricator. He had a grade 12 education, and, fortunately for him, a relative had provided some funds so that he could attend a trade school for two more years of training.

Enoch began to dream of building dishes himself. The mounting pole and sheet metal parts of the dish were no problem for him. But how could he bend the square tubing needed for the ribs and outer rim? The curves had to be correct for the dish to be parabolic and reflect the signal from the satellite.

Taking the only materials available to him, he positioned three bicycle gears horizontally on top of his worktable. With a prayer in his heart, Enoch began to experiment by trial and error, using these simple bicycle gears. He discovered he could ratchet square tubes through this bending device and create correctly bent tubes. Then he welded all the pieces together. Enoch had challenges, but each time he ran into a problem, he thought again about reaching more people with the gospel and prayed God would help him build a good dish. Meanwhile, all unawares, the ATN leadership continued to pray that God would help them find a way to catch Africa's interest.

Enoch prayed and worked his way through the obstacles of manufacturing antenna dishes until he succeeded. When he tuned his first satellite dish, the signal came in strongly.

Finding a friend with a digital camera, Enoch took pictures. Then he went to an Internet café and, after paying a high price, surprised everyone at ATN with the following email:

> Thank you for inviting me to the technician's course in Mwanza. I am very happy that I benefited a lot. . . . Please look at the pictures I have of the eight-foot satellite dish I have made myself. The signal strength is very high and quality level also high at 75–81 percent. They are cheaper and more affordable to many. They are problem-

free. Now many more can benefit from Adventist Television Network. I am ready like as a missionary to share my skills for free to Adventist technicians who have metal work/welding basic skills to construct a low-cost, perfect dish.

ATN leadership was astounded and admittedly skeptical. Bless his heart, but what did a local welder by Lake Victoria know about correctly manufacturing satellite dishes? Would they really work? And what did they cost?

During a visit to Africa, Pastor John Banks and Julio Munoz from ATN met Enoch and evaluated his homemade dishes. They were excellent. The signal quality was as good as or better than that of commercial dishes.

Enoch began to build more dishes, but it was slow work. Soon he built a jig that enabled him to make identical quarter sections of the dish, allowing them to be interchanged. He attached an electric motor to turn the bicycle gears. Now he could mass-produce dishes. Before long, he began to get orders from the churches. Believing the dishes should be built locally, he traveled to other towns and helped our members who had welding skills learn how to build dishes for their locations. The result was dishes of superior quality manufactured locally for less than half the price of commercially produced dishes. Now many more churches got excited and felt ownership.

ATN now employs Enoch full time. God found a man on the shores of Lake Victoria in southern Kenya—a humble welder—to solve the problem of economical dish manufacturing. He is an inspiration to everyone who meets him.

Sharing the blessing

In November 2002, ATN sent Enoch to teach a course on dish building for our churches in Cameroon. While there, he met the team of interpreters from all over Africa. They were doing simultaneous interpretation for the *Amazing Facts* satellite series. The African interpreters saw with their own eyes that Enoch's dishes worked as well as if not better than commercial dishes. They went home inspired and spread the news of Enoch's innovation across the churches of Africa.

Errol Van Eck helped Enoch write a manual about the manufacturing of dishes. Enoch traveled to Zambia, Democratic Republic of the Congo, Uganda, and Rwanda as well as Cameroon, teaching dish-manufacturing courses to hundreds of our brothers. The result? Our lay members are now producing hundreds of antenna dishes in various cities and towns across Africa. In addition, Enoch's training has created a small industry that provides employment for hundreds of Adventist lay people. This has resulted in significant increases in tithes and offerings.

In 2004, church members began securing broadcast licenses and installing low-power television stations (LPTV) to rebroadcast Hope Channel full time in analogue in major cities of Africa. While continuing to train members in dish manufacturing, Enoch is now leading out in the LPTV developments. Through his humble commitment to evangelism and his practical trade skills, God provided a solution to the problem ATN faced in Africa. Enoch is an answer to prayer!

God's providence in providing Enoch Mogusu for Africa is an example of what He is doing worldwide to develop a broad, lay-based movement to use satellite NET evangelism and develop and expand the Hope Channel distribution. The church television network is not primarily composed of paid employees. It is a lay movement bound together by the vision and guidance of the Holy Spirit. Both lay people and professionals have come forward, offering their practical experience, creativity, and expertise in a wide variety of ways for the enlargement of Hope Channel ministry. This commitment and vision is Heaven-inspired. It is a work of the Holy Spirit.

Customs

ATN has conducted satellite evangelism in many countries of the world. For each event, we must ship five tons of very valuable equipment to the host location, and eventually, of course, must return it to California. Customs and importation procedures vary widely around the world. In some countries, regulations are easy to fulfill. In others, a combination of uncooperative officials, mountains of red tape, miles of bureaucracy, and high customs duties make temporary importation of the equipment very difficult or even impossible. We haven't been able to broadcast in some countries.

Preparation for a satellite NET evangelism event begins months in advance. In spite of the best preparation, major difficulties often develop. This chapter shares only a few of the amazing ways God has miraculously opened doors for ATN to conduct these different events.

Manila, January 1999

ACTS 2000—Manila was the first of ten major satellite events It Is Written (IIW) scheduled around the globe. This series of meetings was the dream of the IIW staff, and indeed a very bold initiative. In partnership with many donors and the world Adventist Church, ACTS 2000 would bring a full series of gospel presentations via satellite with multiple language translations to thousands of churches worldwide.

While we were preparing for the first such event, Brad sent us the following email:

> We need the urgent and immediate intervention of God for ACTS 2000—Manila. Here is the situation: The program starts Friday

night, with a test broadcast scheduled for Thursday night. It is now 2:00 P.M. Wednesday. The equipment arrived a week ago Wednesday, and due to holidays we could not start getting it released until Monday. Despite all we have done, we still cannot get the equipment out; we have been unsuccessful. The [Philippine] government is requiring a $330,000 bond for temporary import.

How would God intervene in Manila at such a very late hour?

Pastor Mark Finley and the IIW team, and Adventist Media Productions, along with the leaders and faithful members of the South Asia Pacific regional church headquarters, all prayed and pled for God to make a way. In faith, more than forty churches scattered across the Philippines had installed satellite downlink equipment and were ready for the fourteen-day series. People at other downlink sites as far away as Korea, Japan, Okinawa, Hong Kong, Taiwan, Guam, and Indonesia—where the venue was a fifteen-hundred-seat auditorium in Jakarta Adventist Hospital—eagerly awaited the uplinked event from Manila. And churches across Australia were preparing to record and use the series on a delay basis.

But without the necessary equipment, there would be no satellite series. And now it seemed nothing could happen without the $330,000 bond. This was a monumental amount. The church didn't have this much money to post as a bond.

In this crisis, God had a plan. Through our faithful Adventist pastor who also served as Filipino ambassador to Papua New Guinea, the Honorable Bienvenido V. Tejano, a letter was drafted to Philippine President Joseph Estrada. Ambassador Tejano personally took the letter to the presidential palace late on Wednesday afternoon. The letter requested President Estrada's immediate personal intervention on behalf

Uplink gear released from customs in Manila and on its way

Thousands listen to Pastor Mark Finley in Manila

of the Adventist Church.

Would God intercede through Ambassador Tejano? God's faithful children waited and prayed. They didn't have long to wait. Two hours later, President Estrada issued a letter instructing the Philippine Customs Authority to release the equipment immediately, with no bond. Praise the Lord!

The equipment was cleared quickly, and it was delivered to the convention centre by Thursday noon. But the drama was not over. The next problem was setting up the equipment for our test broadcast Thursday evening. Normally, the technical team wants one to two days to set up, test, and be ready to go. Now there were only hours left. Warren Judd, Colin Mead, Marcelo Vallado, Gerry Betty, Denzil McNeilus, Royce Williams, and our local Filipino team worked very hard to get everything done. By late that same day, they suc-

ACTS 2000 baptism in Manila

cessfully sent a test signal to the sky, and God's people rejoiced! At the scheduled time on Friday evening, ACTS 2000—Manila was on the air, a triumph of heaven against a defeated adversary.

It Is Written reported thirty thousand baptisms from this event.

Ghana, February 1999

Excited by the prospect of ACTS 2000—Ghana, churches in that country were raising money and ordering the necessary downlink equipment. Because their orders made for such a large shipment, local officials were imposing extra taxes, which sent the costs out of reach. It seemed the dream of satellite evangelism would be dashed to pieces.

However, if the receivers could be hand-carried into Ghana as personal baggage, different regulations would apply. This posed the possibility of importing the receivers at a reasonable cost so they could be installed in time for the start of the satellite series. There remained the issue of customs clearance for the equipment arriving with passengers.

"Pastor Mensah, do you think it would be possible to import 130 receivers without paying exorbitant customs duties?" queried Brad.

Pastor P. O. Mensah, president of the Adventist Church in Ghana, flashed his engaging smile and answered positively, "I believe the Lord will make a way. Let us speak with Pastor Joe Hagan." Pastor Hagan, communication director for the church in Ghana, was quickly briefed on the need. He responded in his methodical and deliberate way, "Let me make some inquiries and report back to you as soon as possible."

Could God provide a way? As the leaders worked and prayed about this problem, another crisis loomed. Pastor Phil Follett, General Conference vice president, emailed Warren Judd: "Mark Finley just phoned me. He said that the [production and uplink] equipment is being held in Accra, and the government is demanding a $250,000 bond to get it out. Do you know what alternatives you have in order to solve this problem?"

Precious days—nearly a week—ticked by while the team in Ghana struggled to find solutions. Again, Pastor Hagan was pressed into service to solve the customs bond problem. Our church didn't have the money for this huge bond that needed to be posted.

Quietly Pastor Hagan, along with Pastor Amponsem, executive treasurer for the Adventist Church in Ghana, negotiated on behalf of God's church. And God provided the solution through a sympathetic bank official. "The outcome is that a bank here in Accra has agreed to write a Letter of Guarantee for the $250,000. We are told this will be accepted by the Ghana Customs Authority and the equipment will be released. If all goes well, we should have [everything] on three ADRA trucks tomorrow—Tuesday," emailed Warren Judd.

Meanwhile Pastor Hagan was again busy at the airport, visiting customs officials and devising a plan to import 130 receivers, which were all to arrive one week before the start of the series. To get the receivers to the downlink sites on time, four volunteers from North America hand-carried the receivers to Ghana. Pastor Hagan would meet each person in the baggage claim area as he or she arrived from overseas, and he would clear the shipment with the customs officials. With God's blessing, all the baggage containing the receivers was cleared, and they were distributed on time to the waiting churches.

Pastor Hagan became known as "Mr. Negotiator" as through one crisis after another he patiently and persistently negotiated on behalf of the church. God used him and our church leaders repeatedly. Our church members and the entire team rejoiced at how God opened the way for this successful satellite-evangelism series.

The only people who can fully appreciate the miracle behind this story are those who have experienced the challenges of importing expensive electronic equipment to countries where customs regulations are often made up on the spot and shipments impounded on a whim, and where rates of duty can exceed 100 percent or more of the book value of the equipment. They realize that in these events lies a dramatic answer to prayer!

Tanzania, June 2001

It was exactly one week before the satellite-evangelism series with Pastor Jere Patzer and his team from the northwestern United States was to start. We had allowed ourselves a couple extra weeks because temporarily importing the production equipment involved working with two countries. The equipment had been air-freighted to Nairobi, Kenya, where it was promptly impounded. Getting permission to free the equipment in Kenya was no small task; it took Brad and Warren Judd more than a week of going from one office to another. Finally, the equipment was released on bond.

Several days behind schedule, they were ready to head for Tanzania. Outpost Centers Incorporated Kenya (OCI), with their team headed by Andy and Debbie Aho, supplied the large trucks for the nearly twenty-four-hour drive from Nairobi to Mwanza, Tanzania.

Andy Aho and his workers loaded the more than twenty pallets of TV production gear onto two of their five-ton army trucks. Accompanied by armed guards, the convoy rolled out of Nairobi, traveled to the far western side of Kenya, and finally arrived at the Tanzanian border. Church leadership believed that Tanzanian customs would quickly clear the equipment, but that was not to be.

In fact, the team was shocked when the officials there refused to let them pass. One day dragged by as Pastor Mbwana, president of the Adventist Church in Tanzania, and Brad were shuffled back and forth between offices. The only phone at the border wasn't dependable, yet the border officials needed to communicate with their superiors across the country in Dar es Salaam, which was more than a thirty-six-hour drive away. Fortunately, cell phones worked.

Finally, word came. The equipment would be released only if the Tanzanian government communication minister granted authority to broadcast our event in the country. Previously, church leaders had been told this would not be required.

However, getting this approval necessitated a personal appointment with the national minister of communication. The next day was a holiday, and the weekend was approaching. The satellite-evangelism event was scheduled to start Saturday night. All our careful planning to be ahead of the game was being foiled.

So, Pastor Mbwana phoned Pastor Bina. "Please get on a plane as quickly as possible and get to Dar es Salaam and see the minister of communication."

Pastor Bina asked me to accompany him to the airport. We were at the stadium in the center of Mwanza, about ten miles (fifteen kilometers) of very, very rough roads from the airport, and we had only about twenty minutes to catch the last flight of the day! The 4x4 pitched and bucked as Pastor Bina dodged deep holes in the washboard roads, expertly maneuvering around pedestrians, animals, carts, and other vehicles on that busy afternoon. Faster and faster he drove. Hanging on for dear life, I prayed. When we got to the airport, we rushed to the counter and purchased a ticket, and Pastor Bina got on the flight.

But how would Pastor Bina get an appointment with the minister of communication so late that afternoon? What would he say? It seemed clear that the series would not proceed without a miracle at the very last possible hour. So, everyone was praying for a miracle!

God provided the answer in a quiet, faithful Adventist sister who was a secretary in the communication minister's office. While Pastor Bina was in the air, Pastor Mbwana phoned the secretary. Could she get an appointment? She wasn't sure, but she would try. National government ministers don't often take last-minute appointments just before holidays.

Pastor Bina landed in Dar es Salaam and raced to the government office. The secretary happily told him she had secured an appointment. He was hurried into the presence of the Tanzania minister of communication only moments before the offices closed.

Pastor Bina presented the importance of the international event for the Adventist Church. He pointed out that it would be an embarrassment to the Tanzanian government if the satellite event could not proceed because of customs' red tape.

The minister listened carefully and then asked for his secretary.

"Is this your church?"

"Yes," she replied.

"OK, then we will help. Send a fax immediately to the border granting permission to broadcast their program. Let customs release this equipment. We only ask that we be informed when it leaves the country again."

The shipment was released, and the trucks rolled through the Tanzanian border. The next day the equipment was set up in the stadium, and another NET event was on the air.

Again, God's angels had intervened. Again, the roadblocks had not stopped God's program! The Adventist Church in Tanzania reported thirty-four thousand baptisms from the Africa for Christ series.

Cameroon, November 2002

"Today, we need a miracle from God, or this series will not start as scheduled. Let us earnestly pray for Heaven's intervention, for the evil angels to be pushed back, and for God's Holy Spirit and holy angels to make a way through this 'Red Sea' and give us victory." I quietly spoke with the team members gathered for prayer early Thursday morning only one week from the beginning of Pastor Doug Batchelor's *Amazing Facts* satellite series in Yaoundé, Cameroon.

Several months before, the production and uplink equipment had been shipped by sea container and had arrived in ample time at the seaport of Douala, Cameroon. We were really going to be ahead of the game this time! All the paperwork was in order (so we thought) and in the capable hands of ADRA director Andrew Njoke, who had spent the last ten days in Douala, patiently shuttling from one office to another.

Mysteriously, it seemed something was missing, but we couldn't identify what the problem was. Each day Andrew would report to Warren Judd in Yaoundé. Time zone differences complicated the whole process. Warren would have to wait until late in the day to call the shippers in California. Each minute of the international phone calls cost nearly ten dollars. Then, during the night, a fax of more information would come, and the next day

Warren would present these new documents to the officials in Douala. Because of the time change, a day was lost every time an official asked for another piece of documentation. It was very frustrating!

Finally, Warren contacted the head office of the international shipping company located in Switzerland, which at least was in a time zone closer to that of Cameroon. Soon he reached the correct department and spoke to a supervisor. This woman listened to the saga he presented. We had prepaid for the delivery of the container in California, and yet the receiving company in Douala was insisting that the entire amount be paid again.

Within a half hour, the woman discovered the problem. A wrong waybill number had been assigned to our shipment. Impossible! How could our shipment have traveled all the way from California, passed through several different shipping companies, on two different ships, and have had the wrong waybill tracking number all along? It was amazing that the container had arrived at all, but this is exactly what had happened. Once the head office got the correct waybill number, they sent a fax to Douala. They were requiring only a small deposit to assure that the container would be returned. Colin Mead caught a bus and traveled Thursday night to Douala with the money.

Three more things needed to happen and with not a moment to spare if our NET series was to start on time. First, the shipping company had to release the container. Second, customs had to clear the shipment. Third, we had to have the container in Yaoundé by Friday. The trucking companies didn't operate on Sunday, and Monday was a national holiday. If the shipment left on Tuesday or later, our technical team wouldn't have time to set up and be ready to broadcast by our deadline the following Thursday evening. So, we had to get the container out that Friday.

Thank God, a faithful Adventist brother was in the customs office in Douala. He had been briefed on the shipment and the tight deadline. Within a half-hour of the shipping company releasing the container, this brother had the paperwork completed and stamped, allowing the importation of the goods. God had made a way again, answering our pleas for His help. We secured a truck and left Douala on Friday with our container of goods.

In Yaoundé, one last challenge confronted us. Warren called me and told me what it was. "Kandus," he said, "we need a crane that can handle at least twenty-five tons. It must meet this truck and take the container off today, as the truck must return to Douala."

Quickly, our church leadership pointed me in the direction of the only crane company in the city. Praying, I went straight to the office and asked to speak with the manager.

"I'm very sorry we are unable to assist you at this time," he said. "Our crane is broken down, and there are no parts for it in the city. We cannot help you."

Interesting! How was the Lord going to help us out of this new predicament? As I stepped out of the office, a man who was waiting in the reception area and had overheard the conversation followed me. He said he knew of a private company in the city that had a crane.

Now the questions were Could we reach them? and Was their crane big enough to do the job?

More prayers, more phone calls, more anxious moments, and finally we located the owner. He said his crane wasn't big enough, but he would try to help us.

Hours later, the truck rolled in to the stadium, followed by the crane. Gingerly, the skillful operator lifted one end of the container. Back and forth he "walked" the container toward the end of the truck deck. He lowered that end of the container to the ground and attached his cable to the other end. Then he raised that end up, allowing the truck to pull out from underneath the container. It was quite a spectacular feat. Our team watched with their hearts in their throats, all the while praying that none of the equipment was being damaged!

Everything was fine, and we all thanked God for His answers to our prayers of need. Once again, the equipment was ready for setup, and God's program proceeded as planned.

In all these experiences, the miraculous element was that God had strategically placed faithful Adventist members who were the right people, at the right time, in the right place to influence and assist His church when needed. The success of these satellite-evangelism events can be largely attributed to these dedicated members. As in the times of Esther, Daniel, and other Bible heroes, these modern believers were willing to allow the Lord to use them to advance His work. Because of the series, ninety-two hundred new believers joined the Adventist Church in Cameroon and thousands more in other countries.

Host Venues

ATN has conducted nearly ninety satellite-evangelism NET events to date. A key to the success of a satellite NET event is the host location. Ideally, the host location provides an attractive venue, an enthusiastic audience, and the technical infrastructure to conduct the meetings. Typically, a lot of thought, discussion, and prayer go into the selection of the host site. Legal contracts are established for the chosen venue several years in advance.

In most situations, we've had no problems in using the host-site facilities. Occasionally, however, despite the best possible preparations, unusual difficulties develop, necessitating divine intervention to solve the problem. The following stories recount the miracles that God has performed to provide locations for satellite-evangelism events.

Italy, February 2000

Adventists in Italy wanted very much to broadcast the Italian NET satellite series from Rome. Because Rome is the capital of the country with the largest population of any city in Italy and because of Rome's rich heritage in Christian church history, a NET series from that city would have special significance. But where could the planners find a suitable host location? Rome is one of the most secular cities in the world, and its religious culture has not been particularly open to the Adventist message.

Pastor Paulo Benini, leader of the Adventist Church in Italy, and his fellow leaders and church members prayed for God to lead in the selection of a host venue. As they explored various possibilities, someone asked, "What about the beautiful Waldensian church in the center of Rome?"

This church is in an excellent location. In the heart of the city, it is a well-known historic landmark. Its simple, elegant design and décor personifies the dignity of Christian nobility. Would the Waldensian leadership be open to this idea of their church being the host site for an Adventist NET series?

Through the centuries, the Waldensian people of Italy have championed Bible truths. They've been "keepers of the flame," preserving truths that the forces of apostasy wanted to extinguish. Adventists have admired the integrity, bravery, and faith of these heroes. We've built and maintain a special friendship with the Waldensian Church.

The Waldensian church in Rome from which the Italian series was uplinked

Together, Pastor Benini and Brad visited the Waldensian church and met their leaders. Surprisingly, these people were quite open to the idea—and, in fact, intrigued that they could be part of such an innovative way of preaching the gospel.

The only potential problem was finding a place to site the uplink equipment. High buildings all around blocked line-of-sight access to the satellite. The only option was to place the dish high on the roof of the church. But the Waldensian leaders gave their OK. "If you can get your equipment up there with no damage to our church, it is fine with us."

When the time for the NET meetings arrived, getting the equipment up on the roof proved to be more of a challenge than anticipated. The heavy cases had to be hand-carried up a tall, winding, and narrowing staircase. Just getting the equipment up onto the roof took eight hours.

The roof was so steep that a special scaffold had to be built to hold the dish. The resulting platform was still very small; there was enough room to aim the uplink dish in only one direction. Providentially, it was just right to "see" the satellite.

On opening night, the Jubilee 2000 NET series with speaker Pastor Ianno was broadcast to all of Europe and the Pacific Rim. The signal was uplinked from the precarious location on the roof, passing directly over the Vatican City St. Peter's Basilica less than a mile away, to the satellite and then to all of Europe. The kind hospitality of the Waldensian church for this special series was a providential blessing from heaven.

Brazil, April 2000

Pastor Erlo Braun was the pastor of two churches in the city of São Paulo. In November 1998, he contacted Pastor Henry Feyerabend, who was working in Canada, and invited him to be the speaker for a Brazilian satellite series in April 2000. The local area Adventist church leaders were not too sure about hosting a satellite series. NET '98 with Pastor Nelson had been interesting to follow, but could a local conference produce their own series? Pastor Braun was sent to the central Brazil church headquarters to pitch the idea. Maybe they would catch the vision and see the potential.

The leadership of the Adventist Church in central Brazil listened carefully. Yes, they would support a satellite series. Pastor Edson Rosa was appointed satellite coordinator, and Esperança 2000 was born.

But where could the series be hosted? The Vila Formosa area of São Paulo is a very difficult neighborhood for evangelism. The people are very traditional and not open to discovering new Bible truth. And the Adventist church was very small—too small. Pastor Braun combed this area searching for a suitable venue. There weren't many options. As he continued to search, he prayed that God would provide. Then he discovered a Baptist church in the right area. He approached the leaders of that church. Would they be interested in renting or selling? After discussion, prayer, and negotiation, rental and purchase prices were agreed upon.

"Buy the Baptist church? Impossible! I'm sorry; we have no funds for such a purchase." Pastor Braun pondered the church treasurer's words. It was true; the church didn't have the money to purchase another property. But there were several very good reasons to buy the church. First, they needed a location from which to host Esperança 2000. Second, if they rented it, the rental monies would be expended with nothing to show at the end of the series. Then too, where would the new members go after the satellite event? They would need a church home. So purchasing the church seemed the only solution—there was no other reasonable option.

With the treasurer's words ringing in his head, Pastor Braun went back to his congregation. Vila Formosa was a small congregation of around one hundred members. They listened carefully as Pastor Braun presented the options. The rental price amounted to a third of the purchase price of the property. The Baptist church was in an excellent location. Their congregation had dwindled. Now, many of the members were elderly, and for a number of years they had done very little maintenance on the building. It would require extensive remodeling, but when finished, it would make an excellent Adventist church home. But time was certainly of the essence.

Pastor Braun and his congregation prayed for a solution. Then Pastor Braun had an inspired idea. Why not offer to trade churches with the Baptist congregation and only pay the difference in the value of the properties?

The renovated Vila Formosa church, site of the Brazilian series

The Adventist church would be a good size for the Baptist congregation, and, if renovated, the Baptist church would be an excellent host site for the satellite event. Would the Baptist church members accept such a proposal?

Prayerfully, Pastor Braun approached the Baptist leadership with the plan. The Baptist members seemed very happy with the opportunity and the proposal. Quickly, the lawyers drew up the legal documents, and soon the Adventist Church owned the old Baptist church. But the building still needed very serious repairs—actually, a major renovation—to be suitable to host Esperança 2000.

What happened in the next forty-five days was nothing

short of a miracle. Pastor Braun and the Vila Formosa Adventist congregation worked very hard to prepare their newly acquired church for the satellite event. Among the Adventist members were talented carpenters and practitioners of just about every trade necessary. Day and night, the sounds of hammers and saws could be heard as they renovated the sixteen-thousand-square-foot (fifteen-hundred-square-meter) church. People who lived near the church stopped in, commenting on the beehive of activity and the positive changes.

Would they make the deadline in time for the broadcast of the satellite series? With God's blessing and many more amazing providences and miracles, the Vila Formosa Baptist church received a complete makeover inside and out, with the final touches being added the very day the series began.

The experience of the Vila Formosa church strengthened the faith of other Adventist congregations in the Central Brazil region. Nearly two thousand churches were equipped with satellite equipment to participate in Esperança 2000 from the special host site God providentially provided. The acquisition and renovation of the Baptist church also seemed to ignite the spirit of the Vila Formosa church members. And the Lord blessed their hard work and faith, nearly tripling their membership.

Cameroon, November 2002

Planning for the Visions for Life series had started about eighteen months in advance. As always, selection of the host site was crucial. There are only about five thousand Adventist members in Yaoundé, a city with a population of 1.5 million, and none of the Seventh-day Adventist churches were large enough to accommodate the anticipated attendance.

After much discussion, organizers selected the national stadium as the host site for this evangelistic series. The stadium is a large and popular venue that had never before been used by any religious organizations despite frequent applications. Pastor Emmanuel Nlo Nlo and Pastor Jean Marie Tchoualeu, along with other leaders from the Adventist Church headquarters in Cameroon, approached the government. After a lot of prayer and a number of discussions with various government officials, the president of Cameroon himself granted the Adventists permission to use the national stadium.

"We have a very serious problem in Yaoundé. The government has withdrawn their promise that we can use the stadium, and there is no other facility suitable or available at this late date to host this series. We must find an immediate solution. Do you have any ideas for us?" I could hear the anxiety in Pastor Gary Gibbs's voice. Amazing Facts had invested a lot in the upcoming NET series in the Cameroon. As vice president of Amazing Facts, Gary was responsible for the overseas evangelistic meetings Pastor Doug Batchelor held—and this event was facing a serious crisis.

With less than a month to the start of the satellite series, the pressure started from sports officials. They wanted to hold their annual soccer tournaments in the stadium. After all, it was the 2002 CAF (Confederation of African Football) Cup, and Cameroon had once again made the finals.

To understand the importance Africans accord soccer, think of combining all the enthusiasm of North Americans for the sports of football, baseball, and basketball. Soccer is very important to Africans, and each year a very large television audience in every African country follows the CAF cup games. There was no way the Cameroon government would pass up the opportunity of hosting their championship games in their own national stadium. Certainly, no church and no commitment of even the president himself would stand in the way of the CAF games.

What could be done? The series had to proceed. Across the continent of Africa, Adventist congregations were preparing for the satellite-evangelism event. People had expended considerable effort and finances in preparing for the series. The production and uplink equipment had been on a ship for three months and would be arriving at any time. So, church officials in Africa and the leaders at ATN and Amazing Facts engaged in serious discussion and prayer.

The only viable option seemed to be to approach the stadium officials and request permission to share the stadium with the sports crowd. The soccer games always took place in the afternoon, and the satellite series was planned for the evening. Perhaps the two events could coexist in the same venue. Would the Cameroon government agree to such a proposal? It was a long shot, but worth pursuing. Some of our church leadership was hopeful, and there were several influential Adventist members. Perhaps they could move the authorities to favor our proposal.

Two weeks before the start of Visions for Life, I arrived in Yaoundé to assist the local church in making final preparation for the event. Pastor Gabriel Boakye-Dankwa, Warren Judd, and I walked through the stadium and decided what we would request. Our production and uplink equipment room would have to be secured. We could design the stage, backdrop, and large screens so they could be taken down after the meeting each evening and then set up again the following day after the games. It would be hard work and require a lot of personnel, but it was doable, so this was what we would propose. We all prayed earnestly for God to intervene and provide a way.

During the meeting with the stadium manager, we explained our need and the plan we thought could work. We didn't really expect the management to accept our proposal, but in faith we asked for everything we possibly could. Then we walked through the stadium with the management personnel, and I described the layout we wanted and the things that would need a permanent location throughout the series. As we did so, we heard the manager say to his assistant, "Whatever these people want—whatever their wishes—accommodate them."

We were ecstatic. This was a miracle! It was the first time any church had used the national stadium, and for us to be there during the soccer championship gave our series outstanding publicity. In fact, the 18' x 32' (16 x 12 meter) baptismal tank on the edge of the soccer field was a continual visual symbol of God's will. Indeed, God had provided a way!

To our great surprise and joy, we learned only later that the stadium manager was an Adventist who had not been attending church for some time. When God's people had a crisis, miraculously, God had a person in position to assist so that what seemed impossible could be accomplished.

Nigeria, November 2003

The Enyimba Stadium in Abia State, city of Aba, was the host site for the Visions for Victory satellite NET series hosted by Global Evangelism and the West-Central Africa Division. Pastor Don Schneider, president of the North American Division of the Adventist Church, was the speaker for this series. The church contracted for the use of Enyimba Stadium for a three-week period for the satellite series. However, prior to the start of the meetings and again after the opening weekend, some very unusual events indicated that a greater "game" was being played there—a match that was part of the great controversy.

"Pastor Dankwa, if this is where the stage is to be, that light pole will have to be moved." Pastor Dankwa was giving me my first tour of the venue for the series. It was a very nice stadium. In the past, the Enyimba Stadium had never been rented to any religious organization. In fact, it took the president of the Enyimba Football (soccer) League a whole month to think over the request before he graciously signed the contract permitting Visions for Victory to be uplinked from this state-owned venue.

When only one week remained to the start of the satellite event, a lot still needed to be done. The stage had to be completed. Some of it had been prebuilt but would need assembly on site. But now a huge light pole, with a rack of twenty-seven stadium lights, lay on the track exactly where the large stage was to be set up. This was a problem.

The very next day the national football team was to play an international game, and we were assured that the light pole would be installed in time for this game. However, that Friday afternoon as we stood in the grandstand surveying the stadium, the heavens opened with a torrential tropical rainstorm, leaving the track muddy and impassible. There was no way now for a crane to drive onto the field to set up the pole.

For six days, our group was promised the pole would be moved. But no amount of negotiation, discussion, or even prayers could seem to get a crane into the stadium—or even the necessary federal government permission to move the pole. The pole still lay exactly where the stage was to be set up, almost as if the devil had said, "Just try to have an evangelistic program!" On day six, with only three hours of daylight left, there was still no crane in sight.

Moving the light pole for the Nigerian series

As precious minutes ticked by, miraculously, a crane was sourced and released, a driver for the crane secured, and the crane rolled into the stadium. Within a short time, the light pole was safely shifted out of the way with no one injured and with no damage to the light pole. Just as the sun set on the final night before the start of the evangelistic event, the heavy stage was moved into position and the Adventist Media Productions crew positioned the lighting for the stage. It was truly a victory for Visions for Victory.

But a greater storm was brewing. After the opening weekend of the meetings, we heard a rumor that the stadium officials were going to ask us to vacate the stadium so they could prepare to host a soccer match in their stadium. After thirty-nine years of frustration, Nigeria was in the Confederation of African Football (soccer) Cup playoffs. Soon the official letter came, giving notice that we were to conclude our program and move all our equipment out within less than five days!

How could we do what they asked? The host audience numbered around six thousand nightly and more than twenty-five thousand on Sabbath. Where would we go? And disassembling, moving, and reassembling nearly five tons of uplink and production equipment would take at least forty-eight hours. The move would interrupt the broadcast schedule for nearly fifteen hundred downlink sites across Africa. Moving seemed almost impossible, and concluding the program six days early was unthinkable.

When we approached the president of the football league by phone, he responded, "There is no room for negotiation. Put any thought of a compromise out of your minds!"

Respectfully but boldly, a local lay member, Dr. Frank Adieleuwa, countered, "My friend, you are in a position to help God's work or hinder it. I think you should pray before you make a hasty decision. Please pray and then call me back."

We went to our knees and pled for Heaven's help. Hours later, the president of the football league invited us to a private meeting in his home. Here we shared with him the magnitude of the satellite-evangelism event for the Adventist Church. We discussed various options that would allow the meetings to continue and challenged him with the reality that he alone was in a position to allow the satellite series to continue. Then we offered a prayer that the Lord's will be accomplished.

Miraculously, the Holy Spirit completely changed the heart of the president of the football league. Within forty-eight hours a satisfactory solution was reached, permitting the program to continue except for the final Sabbath. We praised the Lord for His intervention and the obvious miracle!

Nearly 10,000 were baptized in Nigeria on Sabbath, November 15, 2003

There's another interesting facet of this whole drama. Prior to these football matches, supporters of the local team practice *juju* ceremonies in the dressing rooms and on the football field, invoking a curse on the opposing team and a blessing for the home team. (In southern Nigeria, *juju* refers to ghosts and evil spirits.) This is an important traditional preparation ritual, and the stadium officials admitted that with the church people and our program in the stadium, they couldn't carry out their *juju.* We told the president of the league and the stadium officials that we believed the Lord was stronger than *juju,* and we prayed with them.

Indeed, God was stronger! Across Nigeria, 9,247 precious souls were added to God's family the last Sabbath. Each baptism was a testimony to a God who is still in control and whose work will continue in spite of apparently insurmountable obstacles.

And not only was the Visions for Victory satellite series uplinked in its entirety, but the national football team also experienced victory!

Uplinks

Funnels come in many shapes and sizes. They capture a wide stream of materials, bringing everything to one central point for distribution. In satellite NET evangelism, the narrow part of the funnel is the satellite uplink. On one side of this funnel is the evangelist/speaker, all of the program preparation, all of the local volunteers, the translators, the production equipment, and the technical crew. When the program begins, the digital datastream passes through one small wire going to the uplink equipment, which sends the digital data to the satellite that then distributes it to the thousands of churches and often hundreds of thousands of viewers around the world.

Obviously, the uplink is critically essential! The broadcast and reception of the entire program comes down to one rack of equipment and the dedicated creativity of the engineer. The success of the entire broadcast hinges on this narrow point of the funnel.

The Adventist Television Network (ATN)/Hope Channel network depends on a select group of dedicated individuals who work quietly behind the scenes, usually preferring anonymity. These people are critically essential to the broadcasts. Their ministry is highly technical and creative. They minister with their talents and skills to advance God's work.

Since the engineers have completed hundreds of uplinks for various occasions, they usually face few problems. However, on some occasions, challenges have arisen that have called our staff to pray and forced them to perform under extreme pressure. And God has intervened miraculously. Through His providence, this team has grown. We thank Him for the consecration and vision of our broadcast teams. The following stories recount some of the unusual ways God has guided to solve uplink problems, permitting the success of satellite-evangelism series and programs.

United States, October 1996

It was the first broadcast of NET '96 with Pastor Mark Finley to Europe. The English, Spanish, and Portuguese languages were taped and uplinked directly from the host location in Orlando, Florida. The European translation team was located at Three Angels Broadcasting Network (3ABN), a supporting ministry of the Adventist Church. There the programs were translated into other European languages, recorded, and then broadcast to Europe the following day. Weeks before, in preparation for this event, 3ABN had installed a new encoder, making possible the broadcast of multiple languages.

"Brad, I'm not sure of one thing. I need to check something before the uplink starts—I'll be right back." With that, Moses Primo dashed outside to the small uplink building. Brad looked down at his watch. It was just a couple minutes to the first broadcast of NET '96 to Europe. *This is getting really close!* he thought as he wiped his sweaty palms and breathed another prayer for God's blessing on Moses. *Is this really going to work?*

In the final days before the transmission, Moses and his team had carefully hooked up a myriad of cables for the new encoder, and had checked and rechecked everything. Now, just moments before the broadcast was to begin, Moses was once again methodically reviewing the wiring plan for each language. Slowly, the seconds ticked by and the room filled with tension. Then, Moses, breathless, returned.

Five, four, three, two, one!—exactly at the scheduled time, Moses pressed the switch, and the program went directly to Europe. Scott Grady, at the audio mixer board, monitored each language channel to confirm the audio levels. And tears came to Brad's eyes as he witnessed the modern-day fulfillment of the miracle of "speaking in tongues" that had started with Pentecost so long ago in the New Testament church. It was so exciting to hear all the different languages! This was a historic moment for the Adventist Church.

Picking up a phone, Brad called the Stimme der Hoffnung media center in Darmstadt, Germany, and spoke with Stefan Fraunberger.

"Stefan, are you getting a good quality signal?"

"Yes, it's coming through strong and clear!" responded Stefan.

"Wonderful! Let's check the language channels."

In Europe, one by one, each language was checked and verified. Brad could hear the voice of each translator over the phone as Stefan checked the languages on the studio monitors.

"Praise the Lord! Stefan, this is really working! Amazing! This is a new day in the Adventist Church!" This was the first digital broadcast of satellite NET evangelism. Digital broadcasting allowed for larger numbers of languages to be broadcast.

After the broadcast, Brad, the translators, Moses, and the 3ABN technical team gathered to pray, thanking God for the success they had just experienced.

For nearly a year, intense work had been done to prepare for this moment on the assumption that digital multilanguage broadcasting would work. One must remember that in 1996, the Adventist Church of North America was using analogue broadcast for satellite evangelism. The NET '96 multilanguage transmission was the first digital broadcast of this nature for the church. The church of Europe had stepped out in faith. A very large investment had been made. Thousands of church members had worked intensely in preparation. Through the donations of generous, dedicated church members in North America, 3ABN had committed to provide the encoder and broadcast.

NET '96 demonstrated to the world Adventist Church that broadcasts could be made globally in multiple languages. Digital technology (which ATN uses exclusively today) showed huge potential for both satellite evangelism and, ultimately, the direct-to-home TV broadcasts of the Hope channels. This significant step laid the foundation for the world church Adventist Television Network.

God led and confirmed His guidance through the results of this event. It Is Written estimated that more than fourteen thousand individuals joined His family through NET '96.

Brazil, December 1998

The Adventist Church in Brazil is vibrant and dynamic. It began to catch the vision of satellite NET evangelism early on. South America practices "integrated evangelism," which means that all activities of the church focus on evangelism. So, when Pastor Bullón was scheduled to broadcast a series of satellite NET meetings from the city of Belém, Brazil, in December of 1998, hundreds of churches began to install dishes and prepare for the meetings. Members prayed, gave Bible studies, and conducted small-group meetings.

The ATN headquarters in Brazil are located at Novo Friburgo, near Rio de Janeiro. Wanting to keep expenses down, the personnel decided to truck the equipment to Belém, a drive of about 2,200 miles (more than 3,500 kilometers). This would take some time, but the roads are good, and the cost of driving would be considerably cheaper than that of airfreight.

Everything seemed to be in order, including the uplink and broadcast plans. But as the time for the meetings to begin drew near, Pastor Williams Costa, Jr., became strangely uneasy about the event. "I just feel something is wrong. I don't know what it is; I've never felt this way before," he told his wife, Sonete.

As Pastor Costa listened to the weather reports on the evening of the day when he had mentioned his anxiety to his wife, he realized his anxiety focused on the long road trip to Belém. There was a possibility of heavy rains along the route. Maybe they should leave a day or two early. He shrugged off his apprehension and retired for the night. But he awoke the next day more concerned than ever. Why should he feel this way? Rain along that route was normal. The highways were good. What cause was there for concern?

Calling Jorge Florencio, the uplink engineer, Pastor Costa asked him to pack the gear and prepare to send it by airfreight.

"Why, Pastor?" asked Jorge. "There's no reason to airfreight this equipment. I will be happy to drive it to Belém, and we will arrive in plenty of time. It will save lots of money if I drive."

"I don't know, Jorge, but something is telling me that we should ship by air. It will be the best," replied Pastor Costa.

Hesitantly, Jorge went to work, and in a few hours he had everything ready to go. In due course, the shipment arrived in Belém.

Just before the meetings began, the headlines on the TV and in the newspapers reported a terrible mudslide on the very road Jorge would have traveled. He wouldn't have made it through the area with the equipment and might even have been in danger. If the equipment had not been airfreighted, there would have been no uplink and no satellite series. God foresaw what was going to happen and guided Pastor Costa to make the right decision.

Church leaders in Brazil reported that nearly eighteen thousand people were baptized and joined God's family from this mighty satellite-evangelism program.

Ghana, February 1999

The technical and production team were busy setting up for ACTS 2000—Ghana with Pastor Mark Finley and the It Is Written team. For a number of days, they wrestled with major challenges. The churches had ordered their equipment quite late, and so the team had to locate nearly 116 more sets of equipment. The IRDs were being flown in as accompanied baggage with four volunteers from North America. But the biggest and most unexpected challenge was with the actual reception of the program.

In an email to Peter Bretherick in Johannesburg, South Africa, Brad wrote:

> We urgently need your help to resolve a reception problem we are having in Western Africa. What puzzles us is why Nigeria, which is not that far away, is getting such excellent results [while] here in Ghana the reception is only marginal . . . at the start of our evening program. Earlier in the day and later in the evening, Ghana has good reception. This whole event in Ghana is quickly turning into a disaster for this local constituency. There are a total of 116 new church sites, and when they cannot get the program, you can imagine the feelings.

This was a significant crisis, and we had to find an immediate solution. The NET meetings had begun. Thousands were filling the churches in Ghana and waiting for the program. We were in trouble!

The satellite used for the event was PAS 4, which was located high over the Indian Ocean but was low on the horizon for Ghana. The frequency assigned to us on this satellite had transmissions on both sides. Consequently, we couldn't purchase more bandwidth to allow for more power, which would have largely resolved the reception problem.

With the help of Peter Bretherick, we finally discovered the reason why the signal strength and quality dropped so mysteriously each evening. It was a tropospheric phenomenon known as scintillation, which can affect one part of a region and not another and which particularly affects signals coming from satellites low on the horizon.

The members of the technical team were in a tough position. They hadn't known about this problem before the series began. This was only the second satellite NET evangelism event for the continent of Africa, and many were still dubious about satellite ministry. Naturally, we wanted to help the churches have a successful series and not lose the investment they had sacrificed so much for. We needed to build the confidence of our members and church leaders, and we had no time to lose.

The only solution was to find a satellite that was higher in the sky. However, changing satellites in the middle of the series and retuning more than 130 dishes hundreds of miles apart all over Ghana would be a huge task. So, there was an intense discussion. It concluded with the decision to secure a second satellite: PAS 3, which was located over the Atlantic. We hadn't budgeted for this expense, but It Is Written graciously agreed to carry some of the cost in partnership with ATN. Fortunately, even with no advance booking, space was available on PAS 3.

We broadcast the next program on two satellites, PAS 3 and PAS 4. As soon as the churches in Ghana aimed their satellite equipment toward PAS 3, they received a strong signal. So, we dispatched technical teams to help the churches point their dishes toward PAS 3.

It Is Written estimates that across Africa this satellite NET event brought forty thousand precious people into God's family. It also built confidence among our African churches regarding this evangelistic tool.

United States, October 1999

"You got to be kidding! How could the shipper be so careless? Man, I don't know if this stuff is going to work!" Marcelo Vallado, Adventist Media Production (AMP) engineer, felt a knot in his stomach. He couldn't believe his eyes.

He'd just flown into New York City from Santiago, Chile, where he'd set up the uplink for ACTS 2000—Chile. Only a couple days were available for him to do the same for Pastor Doug Batchelor's NET '99 New York City series. Then, from New York, he had to fly to Germany to assist in the uplink setup for the first German-produced NET evangelism program. His schedule was very tight.

Now, he was facing a problem. The case containing the big encoder was smashed. It had been dropped from a forklift. Even if the equipment inside was in one piece, the fact that it had sustained an impact strong enough to destroy the specially designed travel case probably meant that the delicate electronic equipment inside had suffered serious damage. Without a functioning encoder, there would be no uplink.

Quickly, Marcelo set up the uplink dish and the up-converters on the roof. Even before the equipment was damaged, he'd been concerned about this uplink. He faced major restrictions: The city places restrictions on the frequencies for uplink. High skyscrapers block access to many satellites.

And on this particular building, production was seven or eight floors below, which necessitated a very long cable running from the encoder to the uplink dish. This also could create problems.

When the dish was ready, Marcelo went down to the production area and began setting up the encoder. Would it work? The last time the encoder had been used was earlier that year in Ghana, where the broadcast was in the PAL video format. For the New York event, he would need to switch the encoder back to the NTSC format. Normally, this does not take long, but on that day, the encoder wouldn't switch. Hour after hour he worked. The problem was that the computer wouldn't communicate with the encoder. Obviously, something had been damaged in the accident—but what?

Carefully and systematically, Marcelo began to go through all the video cards in the encoder. Finally, he called the office of the manufacturer. An engineer joined him via the phone, and together they went through numerous possibilities. After resetting the network card and troubleshooting the long cable, everything was ready for the broadcast.

Marcelo was exhausted and he hadn't eaten for hours. There was still a lot to do, but he and the rest of the technical staff went to get some food. Upon returning, Marcelo discovered, to his horror, that in the short time they'd been away, someone had broken into the encoder room and stolen his briefcase. That briefcase contained both his personal computer and the system computer used to operate the encoder! Now he had no passport, no tickets for his trip to Germany, and no computer with which to run the encoder for the test broadcast scheduled for later that evening. In a short time, hundreds of churches across North America were expecting to tune in to test their equipment. Marcelo had to be on air!

He glanced at his watch. The test broadcast was supposed to begin within an hour. The encoder operates like a computer, but it needs a master computer as a server to control all the functions. Marcelo sent Terry Cantrell, a team member, to buy another computer, but he realized he might not have enough time to configure the new computer. So, with a prayer in his heart, he decided to do something he had never done before. He decided to see if he could override the network and manually control and operate the encoder.

Marcelo worked right up to the scheduled slate-message time, and, amazingly, he got the encoder to function without a master computer! It sent a strong signal to the sky. In less than twenty-four hours, God had helped him overcome damaged gear and the theft of the master computer that operated the encoder and begin the broadcast of another satellite NET evangelism series. No one across North America even knew the difference!

A few hours later, someone from the company that provided security for the building found Marcelo's passport and airline tickets several floors below in a garbage can in one of the bathrooms. Marcelo traveled on schedule to Germany for the next satellite-evangelism event, which began the following weekend. In less than three weeks, he had worked on three different continents and God had helped him launch three major NET series. It Is Written, Amazing Facts, and our church in Germany estimate that these three events resulted in the baptism of more than fifteen thousand people.

Scotland, March 2002

It was just days before the uplink of the Ministry Professional Growth Seminar from Edinburgh, Scotland, led by the General Conference Ministerial Association with Pastor Jim Cress and Pastor Nikolaus Satelmajer. The University of Edinburgh owns historic McEwen Hall, the chapel from which the event was to be broadcast. When the team approached the university about positioning the uplink dish on the roof of the building, they were met with a flat-out refusal. "I'm sorry; you can't touch this historic heritage building. Setting your equipment anywhere on this building is unacceptable."

Even before this problem arose, Marcelo and Warren had concerns. The look angle to the satellite was bad; the satellite was very low on the horizon, and because tall buildings surrounded the university, they couldn't get a good view of the satellite from anywhere but the top of one of the buildings. Further complicating matters, the uplink dish and equipment must be positioned relatively near the actual production.

Warren and Marcelo didn't know what to do. How would God provide a way this time? As they were walking back from their lunch break, suddenly Marcelo said to Warren, "There's our solution!"

Marcelo pointed to tall scaffolding that stood next to a nearby building and said, "Perfect! We can rent scaffolding and raise the dish as high as needed to see the satellite." They made a note of the phone number on the side of the scaffolding and immediately called the company.

By the next afternoon, the scaffolding was in place beside the historic university building. The team never touched the building; they just ran the cables to the production unit inside. For Marcelo, uplinking took on new heights; from the top of the scaffolding, he had an excellent view toward the satellite.

Edinburgh is famous for the heritage of John Knox, one of the greatest preachers of the Reformation. His opponents feared his preaching more than they feared opposing armies. Around the world, twenty-five thousand pastors of many faiths participated in this professional growth seminar on the theme of powerful biblical preaching.

Perhaps to some, this solution seems a small matter. At the moment, it was a providential answer to a challenging obstacle and another evidence of God's interest in the satellite broadcasts of His people.

Weather

"The wind and the waves shall obey thy will; peace, peace be still." The words of the old hymn could have been the refrain of Adventist Television Network staff as they frequently confronted temperamental, sanguine Mother Nature. Outdoor stadiums have comprised the venues for many of the satellite NET events, and the uplink dish that sends the signal to the satellite is always out of doors and vulnerable. Often, in tropical countries, these exposed settings led to challenges.

Church downlink sites were also vulnerable to weather-related problems. During NET '95 in the state of Maine, one of our churches experienced a blinding snowstorm during a broadcast. Snow accumulated in the curve of the reception dish, obstructing a clear signal, and the picture inside the church became increasingly "snowy." The dish was high on the roof and no ladder was in sight, so the deacons decided to have a snowball fight. Packing the snow into firm, round balls, they pelted the pole and back of the dish, successfully dislodging the snow. When they went inside, they found the picture restored.

Engineer Marcelo Vallado cleans snow from an uplink dish

As ATN traveled the globe helping local churches establish the Hope Channel network, it often seemed that the battle of the great controversy was being waged on a personal basis. Many times, prayer bands and chains of prayer warriors earnestly entreated the power of Heaven to intervene and hold back the adverse weather. We saw God miraculously work to guard these special programs, even in the foulest weather. The following stories recount only a few of God's interventions during challenging weather.

South Africa, 1998

The first African satellite series, Pentecost '98, with Jamaican evangelist Fitz Henry, was being uplinked from Vista University in Soweto, South Africa, at the beginning of the winter season. The countryside was in flames as the residents of Soweto burned the heavy grass and debris to clean the city and surrounding area. Then the wind shifted, and the fire beside the university got out of hand and began advancing rapidly toward the back of the university auditorium, where the broadcast of Pentecost '98 was being uplinked.

"That fire is burning closer and closer, and if it keeps going, it will seriously jeopardize our program and equipment this evening!" shouted one of the staff. Just moments before the broadcast was to begin, and after an urgent discussion, Brad went to the podium and requested every able-bodied man in the host audience to help fight the fires.

Scores of volunteers rallied to the challenge. Wielding coats, sticks, and whatever else they could find, they began to beat at the hungry flames. They lit a controlled backfire and found a water hose to aid the fight. That entire evening, men and boys beat back the fire as the broadcast continued. The evangelistic team realized that had the fire gotten out of control earlier in the day when none of our staff was there, the ending could have been quite different! We gratefully acknowledged that a higher Power had preserved the equipment and permitted yet another transmission of the gospel.

Papua New Guinea, 1998

Sometimes God uses bad weather to keep people together to listen to the gospel. Adventist churches in Papua New Guinea (PNG) participated in NET '98, which featured Pastor Dwight Nelson and was broadcast from Pioneer Memorial Church on the campus of Andrews University. Each night, thousands streamed into the stadium in Lae to hear the messages from the sky. On one evening, however, the public address (PA) system acted up before the program began. It would produce no audio. Frantically, the technical people tried everything, but nothing they did restored the amplifier.

The audience grew larger as the scheduled time for the start of the program came and went. Someone was sent across the city to borrow another amplifier. In the meantime, the people, many of whom were visitors, became restless and grew noisier. Finally, a mass exodus began. At that, our members prayed, "The people are leaving. Please, Lord, help us restore the PA system quickly."

Just as the people were drifting away from the stadium, God answered the earnest prayers of our faithful members in an interesting way. Suddenly, the heavens opened and an unusually heavy rain pounded down. Not wanting to get soaked, people quickly fled to the shelter of the surrounding banana palm trees. Minutes passed as they waited out the storm.

Then, a pickup truck carrying a borrowed amplifier came swerving around the corner and roared into the stadium. In moments, the PA system came to life—just in time for the beginning of Pastor Nelson's sermon. At that same time, the rain stopped. Hearing the familiar voice of Pastor Maliput Darius, the Pidgin interpreter, the people left the shelter of the palm trees and returned to the stadium. Never were God's people happier to see a tropical rainstorm come and go. Heaven must have smiled that day as God intervened with a rainstorm and banana palm trees to keep an audience to hear the message of salvation.

Ghana, 1999

We were in the midst of ACTS 2000—Ghana with Pastor Mark Finley as speaker. This event was being broadcast from the outdoor venue of the Kumasi Cultural Center. It was being shown at approximately seven hundred church sites across Africa and had an estimated viewing audience of more than half a million people.

Moments before a broadcast of a sermon was to start, I stepped into the building used by the production team and announced, "We've got a serious storm headed our way!" Within moments, the beautiful sky painted with the golden hues of an African sundown had taken on a weird, almost green-gray color that spelled trouble. The wind began to bend the coconut palms over, picking up anything lying on the ground and whirling it high up in the air. Angry, dark clouds rolled overhead, and the horizon lit up with lightning as loud cracks of thunder punctuated the eerie atmosphere. Would there be an uplink tonight?

The technical team scurried around quickly, making sure the equipment was protected. Pastor Dankwa stepped to the podium, gave a rousing, warm welcome, and invited the audience to listen to a beautiful choir program. As he spoke, large raindrops created dark spots on his suit. The team put in a tape of an earlier concert, and the music went out on the broadcast. To the viewers, it appeared as if there was a live concert at the host site. The production team covered the unprotected television cameras with large plastic garbage bags that "for some reason," someone had brought from America.

Then it seemed like the heavens had drawn up all the water in the oceans and was now pouring it upon us. Never had we witnessed or experienced such a powerful rainstorm! Adventist youth leaders stood beside each camera, shielding them with large golf umbrellas that again someone had "happened" to bring from America.

Within moments, Colin Mead called out, "We have rain coming in!" Sure enough, to the horror of the technicians, water was running down the walls of the building used for the production room and heading straight toward the production equipment. Suddenly, the roof began to drip water right over the audio mixer. A maze of cables and cords behind the bank of equipment made it impossible to shift anything or to try to contain the water. Warren Judd grabbed a piece of plywood and covered the audio mixer. A short distance away in another building, the translator team huddled in a tight circle with heads bowed. They offered prayers to the Almighty, though the deafening noise from the rain pounding the metal roofing overhead prevented them from hearing each other.

Suddenly, Brad remembered Marcelo Vallado, who was monitoring the uplink equipment that was broadcasting the taped choir program. He ran over

Engineer Vallado and the rain-threatened equipment in Ghana

to Marcelo, becoming drenched to the skin as he did so. Both Marcelo and Brad were aghast. A pipe-framed canopy covered by a heavy tarp sheltered the uplink equipment. But a huge pool of water was forming between the ribs of the framework directly above the equipment. It appeared that the tarp would burst at any moment, flooding the equipment and ending the satellite series. That water above the equipment had to be moved—immediately!

During this satellite series, twenty armed guards from the Ghanaian National Army were on duty around the clock at the broadcast site. Breathing a prayer for wisdom, Brad and Marcelo called for the soldiers and asked them to use the butts of their rifles to lift the canvas and move the water away from the equipment. Gingerly, the soldiers began to "walk" the pool of water slowly to the side of the canopy. *Whoosh! Whoosh!* Again and again, many-gallon streams of water flowed over the side of the canopy. The soldiers continued their efforts as the rain poured down.

At about 7:25 P.M. the rain eased. However, other than the production team and staff, not a soul was anywhere in sight at the host site. The music tape was scheduled to end at 7:30. Would Pastor Finley be able to preach? By 7:30, the rain had eased to a drizzle. The camera operators took their positions.

"Dad, we're getting electrical shocks!" Jonathon Thorp called out. All the members of the camera crew were standing in several inches of water. The electrical cables lying on the wet ground were shorting out, and every time the camera operators touched the cameras, 110 volts of electricity zapped them!

What to do?

Brad's mind raced, trying to find a solution. He had to isolate the camera operators somehow. Remembering some dry clothes in the production building, he raced to get them. He tore the clothes in pieces and wrapped the pieces around the camera controls, providing crude insulation. If the camera operators were careful, they wouldn't get shocked.

Just as the choir tape ended, the program began as usual—except there was no one in the host location. Pastor Finley was preaching to an empty field! By the end of the sermon, more than a thousand people had returned, and during the altar call that evening, nearly three hundred people came forward, committing their lives to Jesus.

After the meeting, the entire team gathered together and thanked God for His blessing. No one outside the host site knew that a torrential rainstorm had nearly destroyed the meeting. The equipment had suffered no damage, and we had found the best use ever made of M-16 rifles!

United States, September 1999

Pastor Williams and Sonete Costa and Pastor Alejandro Bullón, all from Brazil, were in Orlando, Florida, for the first Spanish La Red (NET) satellite uplink series in North America. Hurricane Floyd was on its way to Florida, having left in its wake a path of destruction through the Caribbean. Everyone was fearful—shop owners were boarding up their businesses, and people were stocking up on food and water, preparing for the worst.

"Mommy, what will happen to us? Where will we go if the hurricane hits us here in Orlando?" queried eleven-year-old Laura as she sat on the floor in front of the TV in their hotel room. Sonete looked at her daughter. She also was very concerned. Quietly she responded, "Somehow God will take care of us."

Pastor Bullón and the team gathered together. What should they do? Should they expect their audience to come the next evening, when the weather forecasters predicted the hurricane would pass through Orlando? What would happen to the uplink equipment?

After discussion and prayer, they decided to cancel the next evening's meeting. The team earnestly prayed that the hurricane wouldn't damage the Forest Lake Academy auditorium or the uplink equipment during the entire series.

Pastor Costa recalls, "That night, we asked the Lord to spare Orlando so the series could continue. When I went to sleep, I remember having a deep sense of peace that the Lord would care for us and put His hand over this satellite-evangelism series."

The next morning, the news reporters announced that the hurricane had bypassed Orlando. Pastor Costa believes that the Lord directly intervened, changing the direction of the hurricane to protect the series.

During this event, a special miracle occurred. Twelve years earlier, a man arrived in Orlando, having abandoned his wife and children at their home in Puerto Rico. Prior to the satellite series, this man met some Adventists and began studying the Bible and attending church. At the end of the series, he was baptized in a service that was broadcast.

The man's wife, who had discovered God's truth sometime earlier, was attending the meetings at a church downlink site back in Puerto Rico. You can imagine her shock when the camera covering the baptism zoomed in on the face of the man who had deserted her and their children years earlier! Contact was reestablished between the estranged couple, and eventually they were reunited in Orlando, a testimony to a God who is in the business of rebuilding and reuniting lives through the power of the gospel—even despite a hurricane.

The God of electricity

How often do you hear of God creating electricity to illuminate an entire city block so His people could finish a satellite-evangelism program? It happened in the city of Bloemfontein in South Africa during NET '98. Lightning knocked out the electricity, engulfing the entire city in darkness—except for one location: the crowded Adventist church!

This also happened in Brazil. During Pastor Henry Feyerabend's satellite series, the grid supplying electrical power to the city of São Vincent failed. Here's a thrilling report about what happened then, prepared by the health director of the Vila Margarida church:

> We have been regularly attending Esperança 2000 and enjoying the inspiring messages of Pastor Henry Feyerabend. Last Wednesday, something very interesting happened. It was around 8:45 P.M.; suddenly we heard a noise and then there was no more video or audio. The church was without power; but one minute later, everything started working again normally, and we continued the meeting until [the broadcast] ended at 9:21 P.M.
>
> As soon as we had gone downstairs, we noticed that only the church block had power, and that the entire neighborhood around us was without electricity. The city of São Vincent had a total blackout! On our way home we passed by an evangelical church whose service was in progress by candlelight. We realized then that God had done something unusual in allowing the city block where our church is situated to have electricity so the satellite programme could continue.

Jorge Florencio, uplink engineer for this series, was in the uplink truck at the Vila Formosa church host site in São Paulo. Each evening as he monitored the broadcast, he listened to the program. As the amazing blackout miracle from São Vincent was being shared in a video report, Jorge couldn't believe his eyes! One of the interviewees was his brother-in-law, Huberto.

Huberto was not a Christian. In fact, for years he had emphatically made it clear that he didn't want anything to do with Jesus Christ. Even Jorge's sister felt it was not possible to reach her husband. But Huberto came to the Vila Margarida church and listened night by night to the messages of Pastor Feyerabend via satellite. His heart was touched. He told the Esperança 2000 reporter, "I met Jesus in this series." After the series, Huberto was baptized—a beautiful testimony to the power of the Light of the world who shattered the chains of darkness and sin.

Papua New Guinea, July 2001

The largest attendance at a host location during the first ten years of satellite evangelism occurred in the city of Port Moresby, Papua New Guinea. During this series of meetings, Pastor Mark Finley was called upon to do marathon preaching in order to maintain peace and order in a crowd containing more people than live in many cities. Pastor Royce Williams, evangelism director for It Is Written (IIW), recounted the experience in an email report:

Last night . . . we experienced another blow from the prince of darkness when the entire city of Port Moresby was wrapped in darkness due to a massive blackout about halfway through Pastor Finley's message. Our generator powering the satellite equipment was running, but there was a problem with the stadium audio and lighting. For a period of about 12 minutes, 100,000 people sat in darkness except for a few lights on the platform. Technicians literally ran from place to place, checking, testing, and rolling out emergency wiring. All the time, Pastor Finley stood on the platform and demonstrated a posture of praying which obviously had a major effect on the massive crowd. A blackout can always set the stage for shouting and cries of fear.

A slate message was put up on the satellite to the downlinks, informing [people at those locations] of the technical difficulties. Never have 12 minutes seemed so long, but at last, we were up with the stadium audio and on the satellite again. Fortunately, the satellite company allowed us extra time to complete the program at about 9:15 p.m. But our problems had not ended, as the stadium lights were not restored. What would happen to 100,000 people attempting to leave a dark stadium to stream into a city enveloped in darkness? The police were concerned about civil disturbance and requested [that] the audience be held until 11:00 P.M., when the city felt confident that electricity would be restored.

While the appeal song was being sung at the close of the sermon, a message was given to Pastor Finley, indicating the necessity of holding the crowd for another two hours. Quietly, Pastor Finley consulted backstage with Palmer Halvorsen, the graphics specialist. Quickly, they decided which sermon Pastor Finley would preach—one that he had last used more than four years earlier, in NET '96.

By the time the appeal song following the first sermon ended, Palmer was ready. Providentially, he had brought along the CDs containing the old sermon visuals. But he was worried. Usually, he and Pastor Finley would spend several hours rehearsing the graphic presentation. Could Pastor Finley preach a second sermon with full graphic illustrations without even a review? Palmer and many others from IIW prayed earnestly for Pastor Finley.

Without notes but with Heaven-inspired power, Pastor Finley preached the second sermon. Palmer marveled that the flow of the sermon with the graphic images was smooth. In fact, it flowed together as well as if they had rehearsed. Certainly, God came to the aid of His servants that evening.

A little extra music in addition to the sermon helped fill two hours. Fortunately, the police decided the audience could be dismissed at that point—Pastor Finley was exhausted and not ready to tackle a third sermon! Electrical power was not restored to the city until 2:35 A.M.

Translators

In fulfillment of Jesus' commission to take the gospel to every "kindred, nation, language, and people," Adventists have made a special effort to cross language and cultural barriers. Digital technology opened the door for providing a multilanguage, simultaneous translation of the satellite NET events, and this has become a major feature of the world Adventist Television Network. This organization serves the world church. The people of each culture know best how to reach those of their own people group, so providing multilanguage service is key to serving the vastly diverse world church family. Through satellite NET evangelism and the Hope Channels, ATN attempts to contextualize the gospel.

Key to this special, multilanguage service are the translators. From various backgrounds and representing many nationalities, these dedicated individuals faithfully use their spiritual gift of "speaking in tongues" to communicate with unseen audiences. In our NET evangelism series, the translation area of the uplink scene is always "holy ground." In fact, the translation booths quickly became known as "Pentecost rooms"!

In order to participate in the satellite events, translators travel to foreign countries—which means that they often experience travel difficulties and inconveniences. The local food differs from their own. They may not speak the local language or understand the local customs. They live for weeks as foreigners in a strange country. Sometimes the translators are in physical danger. Many times they're homesick and concerned for their families. Some suffer with malaria attacks, colds, and flu. Sometimes they receive unkind criticism for their efforts. In spite of all the odds, these translators keenly feel the awesome responsibility entrusted to them and,

Pastor Harry Mhando translates into Kiswahili during NET '98

with the power of the Holy Spirit, put their heart and soul into their work.

Simultaneous translation is the most difficult and exhausting type of translation. In the United Nations, translators typically do it in ten-minute segments, alternating on and off. Some people say that one hour of simultaneous translation is as demanding as a full day of work. The translators for the satellite series often translate two hours or more each evening, with no break.

Many of the ATN translators are seasoned pastors and evangelists in their own right. Each day the team prepares with sessions of prayer and study. The translators work in a common area, watching the speaker on individual TV monitors. Can you imagine the cacophony that results from having up to forty speakers in the same room, all preaching in different languages at the same time? Their voices mingle together, and the casual observer might conclude that no one could understand any of the languages. However, with the technology of the small, unidi-

Forty translators gathered from around the world for NET '98

rectional mikes positioned directly in front of the translators' mouths, the audiences hear only the language meant for them.

As the sermon progresses, the translators become completely immersed in the message. Sometimes they wave their arms enthusiastically. Sometimes, during the appeals, they're on their knees with tears running down their faces. Once, during Pentecost '98, we noticed the Setswana translator, Super Moesi, pick up his small TV monitor and shake it as he appealed to his audience far away in Botswana. The translators are the vital link between the speaker and the local audience.

The following stories are some of the unique, providential experiences ATN staff encountered as we saw God at work in a special way to provide for this multilanguage evangelistic service.

Ghana, March 1999

"Gentlemen, if you don't get me back to the Kumasi Cultural Centre on time for the broadcast, I will be in serious trouble. Can you please drive faster?" Pastor François Louw was the Afrikaans translator for ACTS 2000—Ghana. Sitting in the backseat of the taxi, he felt mounting tension. He kept checking his watch and calculating how far there was yet to go. He knew if he didn't make the beginning of the broadcast, a lot of people in South African churches, many of them guests, would be upset because they weren't receiving the Afrikaans translation. He couldn't allow that to happen! After all, the South African church had sent him all the way to Ghana to interpret, not to be out volunteering as a technician.

Pastor Louw is a multitalented pastor. At the time of this incident, he had become quite adept at setting up and tuning satellite equipment, having helped many South African churches to do so. When a crisis in Ghana developed because many churches weren't receiving the test signals from PAS 7, he offered to help retune antenna dishes.

In the ensuing days, he assisted twenty-eight churches to tune their equipment. Each day, he would leave early in the morning and help as many churches as possible. Returning to the hotel, he would grab something to eat, take a quick shower, change his clothes, and then join the translation team as they were bussed to the Kumasi Cultural Centre for a premeeting orientation with Pastor Finley.

Some churches along the Gold Coast a considerable distance to the west of Kumasi were still not receiving the broadcast. Each day a member from that region would ask that someone come and assist them. But everyone was busy; the demands were great from many areas. Eventually, Pastor Louw decided he would do what he could. "Be at the hotel tomorrow at five A.M.," he told the persistent church member. "I'll spend the day helping you."

The next morning the two set out, using public transport. The trip to the area where the churches were having trouble took hours, and Pastor Louw began to worry about whether he'd make it back in time for his meeting. But eventually they arrived, and in a short time, he succeeded in assisting four or five churches. Then, grabbing a taxi, they began their long journey back to Kumasi. It was now midafternoon and past the time to meet with Pastor Finley and the other translators.

After what seemed an eternity, Pastor Louw and the church member reached the outskirts of Kumasi, only to be trapped in bumper-to-bumper traffic. Pastor Louw was becoming quite worried now—the broadcast would begin soon. He urged the taxi driver to take alternate routes and to drive faster.

Then it happened. BANG! CRASH! SMASH! The taxi he was in smashed into the side of another vehicle, totally wrecking the taxi. The driver admitted that the taxi had no brakes. Fortunately, none of them were hurt.

Breathing a prayer of thankfulness for Heaven's protection, Pastor Louw left his host to sort out the problem. He grabbed his installation equipment and hailed the next taxi that came along. And moments before the live broadcast began, hungry, sweaty, and tired, he ran into the meeting site and joined the translation team, getting a list of the night's texts from his friend, the Xhosa translator.

That night the Afrikaans audience quietly listening to the satellite event from Ghana never realized how close they came to not having a translator. Miraculously, Pastor Louw had not been hurt, and the good Lord helped him interpret the sermon even without his Afrikaans Bible!

South Africa, September 2000

"What are we going to do? We have no Portuguese translator, we don't know who is coming from Angola or Mozambique, and the meeting starts tomorrow evening. Do you know anyone here in Port Elizabeth who could step in and interpret so our Portuguese-speaking audience isn't disappointed?"

We had a serious problem. It was Friday afternoon, the Pentecost 2000 series with speaker Dr. Leslie Pollard from Loma Linda University was scheduled to start the next night, and we had no way of communicating with Angola to confirm the arrival of the translator who we understood was coming. The previous satellite event from Ghana had drawn an audience in Angola of some eighty thousand viewers. Though there were few churches that had downlinks, those that did recorded the programs and passed the videotapes along to many sister churches, where crowds followed the meetings on a one- or two-day delay basis. Our churches in Angola would suffer a big disappointment if there were no Portuguese language translation for this series. We had to do something and soon.

Pastor Hibbert thought for a moment and then remembered a man from Mozambique who was not an Adventist church member but whose wife attended church quite regularly. Was his Portuguese fluent enough? Even more importantly, did he have enough theological vocabulary to translate the sermons correctly?

Within hours, Fausto da Silva was located and asked if he would fill in until after the weekend, when we could reach the church offices in Angola. Hesitantly, but graciously, he agreed, and Sabbath evening he joined the group of fifteen translators for the first program of the NET series. We offered extra prayers that the Holy Spirit would grant him the words to use. Never before had he simultaneously interpreted a sermon.

Monday morning brought the news that our church in Angola had not sent anyone. They asked if it would be possible for Mr. da Silva to continue. We talked with him, explained our difficulty, and asked if he would be willing to interpret for the rest of the series. He said that he would do his best. We were all thrilled—and very grateful that in our need, God had provided.

Night after night, Fausto joined the translation team for earnest prayer before and after the broadcast. Night after night, he interpreted Dr. Pollard's message simultaneously, just like a pro. And night after night, the Holy Spirit touched Fausto with the beautiful messages from Scripture. He had never before understood many of these topics. Slowly, his own heart was drawn to Christ and Bible truth. A few months after the series ended, he and his wife were baptized into God's family—converted through his own translation!

Papua New Guinea, 2001

We were in the final week of the Christ 2001 satellite-evangelism event with Pastor Jere Patzer, broadcast from Mwanza, Tanzania, and we were very, very busy. The day after this event ended, *It Is Written* was to begin an ACTS 2000 satellite series with Pastor Mark Finley, broadcast from a host site in Papua New Guinea. The decision had been made to rebroadcast this IIW series to Africa. More than two hundred fifty thousand viewers who spoke Kiswahili had watched Christ 2001, and thousands had made decisions for Christ. ACTS 2000, the event from Papua New Guinea, would help solidify decisions and nurture the new members in Africa.

A last-minute decision had been made for a Kiswahili translator to go Papua New Guinea. Pastor Mika had been selected by the Adventist Church in Tanzania to provide the Kiswahili translation, and he needed a visa. Many nations won't allow foreigners in unless they have a visa. Normally, passengers cannot even purchase tickets or board airplanes for international travel without one. Pastor Mange, president of the Adventist Church in this region of Tanzania, had helped us find someone willing to sell a ticket. But without a visa, Pastor Mika wouldn't be permitted to board the airplane. However, there was no time for the normal visa process. Something unusual had to happen to shortcut the normal government red tape and bureaucracy.

After lengthy discussions, we felt the best possible solution was to ask the government office in Papua New Guinea to authorize Pastor Mika's travel, promising the airline authorities that a visa would be granted on his arrival. Could this be done? Eventually, we reached Pastor Royce Williams of It Is Written in Port Moresby and requested him to have a visa and travel authorization faxed to the Australian High Commission in Nairobi. Pastor Mika could take this authorization and try to board the plane. Pastor Williams promised to do so immediately.

The next day, Pastor Mika went to the Australian High Commission and inquired about the fax that should have come during the night. There was no fax. The flight for Singapore left that evening, it was past office hours in Papua New Guinea, and the next flight was several days later. If Pastor Mika didn't leave that night, he would arrive too late for the broadcast. There was nothing we could do except ask God for a miracle.

"There's no other option. Pastor Mika, you must board today's flight to Singapore if you are to arrive in time. If you don't make it, there will be no Kiswahili voice. Go to the Nairobi airport and speak to the manager of the United Arab Emirates airline. We will pray that you will find favor in his eyes and be permitted a boarding card."

I put down my cell phone and put my head in my hands. Resolving this predicament would definitely take Heaven's intervention. We'd have to race with time to get him a visa and transport him all the way from Africa to Papua New Guinea in forty-eight hours.

Providentially, the United Arab Emirates airline agreed to allow Pastor Mika to board the flight to Singapore without a visa. Once more we gathered in prayer and thanked God for working out the solution thus far. But the battle wasn't over yet. The next day we got a call from Pastor Mika. He was stuck in a hotel in Singapore and still had no visa.

In his Port Moresby Report # 4, Pastor Williams told how the problem was solved. He wrote, "Fortunately there are Seventh-day Adventists in key positions of government here [Papua New Guinea], and finally the authorization was sent to Air Niugini in Singapore. Pastor Mika is arriving this morning, just ten hours before he is to begin interpreting tonight."

So, God's providential guidance provided the way for these satellite NET events to attract even more to the gospel and to strengthen the commitment of new believers. Many of us thanked Him for intervening in a situation that seemed impossible to resolve. Indeed, Heaven was watching over the ministry of satellite evangelism.

Cameroon, November 2002

The Visions for Life satellite series with Pastor Doug Batchelor from Amazing Facts would begin on Friday evening. There were to be twenty-four translators for this event, making it the most diverse satellite-viewing audience to date in Africa. However, it was now Tuesday morning, and we had discovered to our dismay that eight of the translators had no visas. Without these translators, hundreds of thousands of potential viewers would be disappointed.

Seven translators were coming from African countries—Botswana, Zimbabwe, Zambia, Malawi, and Tanzania. In addition, Pastor Robinson from India was also awaiting a visa. To make the trip, each needed a visa. Complicating matters, flights to and from African cities don't take place every day.

While preparing for this event, we had been plagued with an extraordinary number of serious challenges. We had trouble obtaining the use of the national stadium; incorrect paperwork had held up for weeks the delivery of five tons of production and uplink equipment; we had to install two hundred new church downlinks in Cameroon in a two-week period; we needed to obtain government authorization for the American dental and medical teams . . . the list went on and on. It seemed that every time we turned around, another brick wall confronted us. Now we must find a way to bring

Warren Judd and the author coordinate a 24-language broadcast in Cameroon

in these translators, or the success of the series would be seriously jeopardized.

"Sister Thorp, I'm sorry. The Cameroon Embassy in Pretoria [South Africa] has declined all the visa applications for our seven translators." That was the report from Sister Elize Hibbert, far away in the church office in Harare, Zimbabwe. She continued, "They're requiring Yellow Fever vaccination certificates and a letter of employment guarantee from each country for each translator. What should we do now?"

I was shocked. This was bad news! Just the day before, I had sat in Pastor Jean Tchoualeu's office while he called the embassy in Pretoria, explaining the magnitude of the event that the Seventh-day Adventist Church was hosting and the embarrassment the Cameroon government would suffer if the visas were not immediately granted. We thought they had agreed to process the visas. Now they'd said No.

Silently I prayed, "Lord, this is Your evangelism program. What should we do next?" Almost instantly, an idea flashed into my head: Get the Cameroon government to grant visa exemptions. "Yes! Thank You, Lord—that's our only hope."

But where and how and who could do this for the church?

I stopped the organizational meeting that I was sitting in and shared the news from Zimbabwe and the idea of seeking a visa exemption. I asked the group of our church leaders from Cameroon and Abidjan, "Who among our members has connections to someone at a high level here in the government who could help us with such a request?" They consulted together and then told me to talk to Mrs. Pulcherie Tchoualeu.

I left the meeting immediately and went to her home to explain our problem and seek her assistance. Amazingly—no, providentially—Pulcherie was a friend of the general secretary to the minister of police. They had attended Catholic parochial schools as young children, and through the years had maintained a friendship even after Pulcherie became an Adventist.

Pulcherie called this man on his cell phone and explained our predicament. He instructed her to have someone at the church headquarters prepare an official request on church stationery, including the names and passport numbers for the eight translators. Then we were to meet him at his office the following morning, and he would see what he could do.

In faith, we arranged for the passports to be couriered back to the translators in the various countries. They would need them to enter the country if the visa exemptions were granted. Then, the next morning, Pulcherie and I went to the police headquarters. We walked past long lines of waiting people, straight into the general secretary's office. Pulcherie and her friend greeted each other warmly, and then he reviewed our official request. He stamped the request and signed it, and then instructed his secretary to take us to the director of border police.

Sister Pulcherie had other pressing responsibilities, so she left me alone to meet this other government official. Again, I was escorted past long lines of people. Within moments, I was invited into the director's spacious office and given a chair in front of his big desk, but he didn't greet me or even look up at me.

I sat there quietly, but my mind was racing. This was the craziest thing I had ever done. Here I was—a woman, a non-French-speaking foreigner, and a Caucasian at that. This was ludicrous! What would I say? I prayed silently. Then I remembered my devotional study from the book of Acts; I've always loved the holy boldness of the New Testament church. Suddenly, everything came into perspective. This was God's program and God's problem. We had nothing to lose and everything to gain for His work! Peace filled my heart.

Eventually, the director of police spoke to me and asked what the problem was. I explained the importance of the international broadcast for the Adventist Church, how vital the translators were to the whole program, and what the problem was. Then, looking him straight in the eye, I smiled and said, "You, sir, are the only one who can help us. Will you please grant the visa exemptions?" He asked a few more questions and told me to come back in two hours.

Three hours later, I walked out of the office carrying an official document with the presidential stamp and this man's signature. It granted all eight translators permission to travel to Cameroon for thirty days to assist with the work of the Seventh-day Adventist Church. We were overjoyed! Quickly, we faxed the letter to each translator.

Someone from our team, carrying this official document, met each translator at the airport. Each one was permitted entry into the country. Amazingly, they all arrived on the opening weekend—a testimony to a powerful God who directs the affairs of human beings and governments.

As I've pondered this experience, I can never imagine being granted even one visa exemption—let alone eight—even in my home country of Canada, and certainly not the same day we asked for it! Considering the bureaucratic way all governments everywhere in the world normally work, we felt the Lord did something extraordinary to help His church and this particular satellite series.

Personally, I found this experience tremendously faith building. God wants to work with His faithful children to accomplish what from a human perspective is impossible. This is the miracle factor.

Section II: Strategic Developments

NET '98

Pastor Dwight Nelson, speaker for the NeXt Millennium Seminar held October 9 to November 14, 1998, said, "Years from now we will call this series a 'God moment,' a time when He was at work around the globe in ways that we won't understand until eternity." NET '98 was the church's biggest and only truly global satellite campaign. It was broadcast in forty languages and reached people in more than one hundred countries.

In an article in a December 1998 issue of the *Adventist Review,* Jack Stenger described it this way:

> To understand the scope of NET '98, maybe a little math is in order: six continents, 12 satellite feeds, 25 broadcast and production technicians, five cameras, 22 floodlights, 1,500 host site volunteers, 31 programs, 7,600 sites (2,000 in North America), 100-plus countries, millions of potential viewers, one message, one world, one God. All told, a global adventure that brought the Adventist message to a world audience as never before.

NET '98 was uplinked from the beautiful Pioneer Memorial Church on the campus of Andrews University in Berrien Springs, Michigan. The speaker, Pastor Nelson, taught the messages of Jesus in a new and fresh approach. With energy and humor, Pastor Dwight stressed humanity's need for Jesus Christ. His slogan for the series was "A Forever Friendship With God." In the opening night presentation, Pastor Nelson set the NeXt Millennium series agenda: "God is not someone to be afraid of. He's someone to be a friend of." People around the world watched and listened as he shared the message of the gospel and Bible truths night by night, unveiling a Christ who longs to be a friend to all.

The reports and stories from around the world were inspiring and amazing. Pastor Dalbert Elias, NET '98 coordinator for the Adventist Church in the British Isles, summed up the results in an email:

Pastor Dwight Nelson, NET '98 speaker

It has been the best evangelistic series ever.... NET '98 has gone beyond our greatest expectations.... [It has been] amazing for several reasons: Cross-culturally, NET '98 was an outstanding success. The British and Irish churches were evangelistically together. Previously, although the two cultures worked well together, evangelistically, each did its own thing. Now they were sharing the same campaign. This evangelistic harmony alone justified running NET '98.

Accessions from NET '98 are on target to be the best ever. Baptisms from NET '98 are currently running at an average of more than seven per participating church. It only needs the average of three per church to better the annual accession rate in the British Union Conference!

The NET '98 "Feel Good Factor" produced increased tithe returns.... This increase more than covers the extra funding given to NET '98.

Satellite churches discovered a sense of belonging. Equipping the churches with satellite facilities created a sense of belonging to the sisterhood of Seventh-day Adventist churches on a scale unknown before.

In summary, we are deeply grateful for NET '98 for the following reasons:
- For the joyous revival experienced by members
- For the thrill of renewed faith in the wonderful Advent message
- For members who have been moved to rededicate their lives to Christ
- For the members who have recovered a sense of pride in their church
- For the members who have realized the "bigness" of the global church
- For members who have become re-established as Seventh-day Adventists
- For the nonmembers who have seen the Bible come alive in a relevant way
- For the nonmembers who have come back to Jesus after many wanderings in the world
- For the nonmembers who are and will be baptized
- For the excellent resources that can now be used all over our nations in hundreds and thousands of homes, continuing the influence of NET '98
- For the satellite installations that will bring many more programmes to us from around the world
- For the inspiring and uplifting theme: "A Forever Friendship With God"

What Pastor Elias reported was true around the world where members shared in the event.

Internet evangelism

Another enormous impact of NET '98 was the dawn of significant Internet use by the Seventh-day Adventist Church. Of this, Brad wrote in an email,

Due to the visionary and sacrificial commitment of two young Adventist professionals, Darryl and Cheryl Hosford, and their associates, NET '98 had an extensive Internet Web site. This site was an immense help both for visitors seeking information and for churches around the world accessing a variety of organizational information concerning NET '98. We could not have done NET '96 without email. We could not have done NET '98 without the Internet. . . . During the weeks of NET '98, this Web site averaged over 500,000 hits per week.

At the time, the church didn't fully appreciate or even completely utilize the services Darryl and Cheryl were offering. Today, five hundred thousand hits per week may not seem large, but in 1998, for a church evangelistic Web site, it was huge! Internet technology was quite new for the corporate church, and educating people as to how they could use this tool for evangelism wasn't easy.

Night by night, the Hosfords faithfully Web-streamed NET '98 and hosted a chat room for questions and comments. In "Forever Friends," an article in a May 1999 issue of the *Adventist Review,* Ludi Leito shared a great story from Pastor Daniel Duda, ministerial secretary of the Adventist Church in the Czech Republic. In the city of Brno, a group of young punk rockers gathered around a computer each night at 1:30 A.M. to watch NET '98! They set their alarm clocks to awaken themselves—they didn't want to miss a meeting. Soon there were between seventeen and twenty-five young people watching programs and inviting their friends.

Some of the parents of these youth became suspicious about what was drawing them to the computer in the middle of the night. They joined their kids and began to listen to Pastor Nelson too, increasing the number in the group to thirty-seven. Rosta Klima, the young Adventist man who organized the Internet viewing, says that one night even he couldn't believe his eyes. When Pastor Nelson called the audience to give their hearts to Jesus that night, "skinheads, anarchists, punks [were] holding hands together and praying—most of them for the first time in their lives. Normally, these people would not talk to each other on the streets."

In the *Adventist Review* article mentioned above, Jack Stenger noted, "Satellite technology was not the only way NET '98 created a global community. The overwhelming popularity of the NeXt Millennium website meant the evangelistic campaign was the church's most significant Internet event to date."

In 1996, Darryl and Cheryl founded and hosted for It Is Written the first online Discover Bible School. By 1998, their service had grown immensely. With the help of a volunteer team of Bible counselors, they had introduced nearly thirty thousand students worldwide to Bible truths. Far away in South Africa, Heaven would intervene in the life of a young woman. Through Internet technology and NET '98, Eileen Jacobs's life was changed dramatically.

"Please pray for my sister Eileen. I just talked to her, and she has received an invitation in the mail for NET '98," Heather quietly requested of her church friends, Gawie and Marie Louw in Riversdale, South Africa. Heather had been praying for years that the Lord would touch the heart of her younger sister.

Shortly before the beginning of NET '98, Heather had phoned her sister Eileen, who lived some two hundred miles (over three hundred kilometers) away in Cape Town, to invite her to attend the series at a local Adventist church. As they chatted together, Heather realized that Heaven had already answered her prayers. Eileen told her that she had received an advertisement to "watch an international speaker via satellite on Bible subjects." Heather was thrilled when Eileen agreed that she would go to hear Pastor Nelson.

Quietly, Eileen slipped into the Kuilsriver Adventist Church to watch Pastor Nelson live from North America. Because of work-schedule conflicts, Eileen managed to hear only a few of the messages. While at the church, she took note of the name "Seventh-day Adventist" and later searched the Web, wanting to know more about the church and its beliefs.

Eileen completed her first Discover Bible School lesson on October 12, 1998. Darryl and Cheryl assigned her to Bible counselors Nels and Mary Ann Angelin in Collegedale, Tennessee. Eileen finished her online Bible studies, began attending the Tygerberg Adventist Church, and was baptized early in 2000. Today she is active in her church and passionate about Internet ministry. She continues to share her faith and ministers to others via email and the Internet.

Eileen's experience is a beautiful example of blended-technology evangelism—a compelling illustration of what God can do in the varied and united work of His church body. With satellites, fiber-optic lines that cross oceans and continents, and the dedicated efforts of Spirit-filled instructors, sprinkled with the fervent prayers of family and church members, the lost are found and discover the joy of following truth and uniting with God's family!

Someday in heaven, Darryl and Cheryl Hosford will undoubtedly meet many, many folk who have found "forever friendship" through the unselfish Internet ministries of this talented, technological couple.

"Forward on Our Knees"
Pastor Nelson used a slogan that was also the watchword of Drs. John and Millie Youngberg: "Forward on Our Knees." As prayer coordinators for NET '98, they rallied prayer warriors around the globe, bringing new

understanding of the power of prayer. In an article published in the special edition of the *Adventist Review* on March 4, 1999, the Youngbergs wrote:

Eight years of prayer preparation, eight months of weekly prayer agendas, divine worship prayer services on four different dates, 24-hour prayer vigils, and 12 to 25 pray-ers pleading with God each night even as Pastor Dwight Nelson preached to the world—this is the news behind the news of NET '98.

John and Millie Youngberg led the prayer support for NET '98

The Pioneer Memorial Church prayer circle swelled around the world to some 7,600 sites by faithful prayer warriors who believed that nothing is more beneficial than the "effectual fervent prayer" of the righteous (James 5:16).

We were serving the post-meeting meal to the 40 translators . . . when the report came that the signal wasn't going out for the whole Central time zone of the United States and Canada; hundreds of sites had blank screens. Immediately, several prayer warriors dropped everything and went into the command center and prayed. Troubleshooters worked deftly, telephone operators answered frantic calls, and prayer warriors interceded for divine intervention. Scarcely had we finished praying when the good news echoed, "We're back on line!" Then, "Praise God!" . . .

Miracles of faith are still being written.

The Pacific Union *Recorder* of April 5, 1999, shared two interesting stories:

The Hemet church in southeast California tried some innovative approaches to using NET '98, including informal discussion groups following the meeting.

A woman in one of the groups revealed that 20 years ago she had purchased some books from a literature evangelist and the Sabbath message had lingered in her mind. . . . During NET '98, she watched the afternoon telecast on Channel 53, then attended the downlink at the church, and returned home to watch the same program rebroadcast at 9:00 P.M. On February 6, 1999, she was baptized. . . .

Beth Anne Kendricks, who also attended NET '98 at Hemet, said her mother was Mormon and her father Southern Baptist. Her parents raised her in a Quaker church. Her mother, who had recently been a patient at Loma Linda University Medical Center and was impressed by the care she received, suggested that Beth Anne attend the Adventist church. "On my first Sabbath at the Hemet church," Beth Anne said, "I immediately loved it because of the Bible study." On November 13, 1998, she was baptized.

More stories from NET '98

On the last night of NET '98, a woman from the city of Annemasse, France, gave a testimony. During the series, her three-year-old son had accidentally fallen through the window of their apartment on the fifth floor down to the street below while she was out for a ten-minute shopping trip. When she came back, he was lying on the pavement motionless. Medics came and transported him to the hospital. The doctors there were astounded. They couldn't understand why there was no sign of impact on the boy's body.

This woman, from a Roman Catholic heritage, initially thought the holy virgin was punishing her because she was attending meetings where medieval history was prophetically explained. But she kept coming to the Adventist church for NET '98. At the end of the series, she said that the only explanation she could give for her son's miracle was the explanation her daughter gave: "The angels carried my little brother down to the street!" She added that she continued attending the meetings because she couldn't live without God, and she was convinced that God was in those meetings.

In Romania, Christianity suffered during the long, oppressive years of Communism. The Orthodox Church culture also has a strong influence on the Romanian people. The satellite series with Pastor Dwight Nelson from North America offered an intriguing opportunity to explore Bible truths. Pastor Adrian Bocaneanu, the NET '98 interpreter for the Romanian language, took time to translate into English more than seventy stories received from Romania and Moldova during the series. Two of these stories follow.

One woman who lived in Barasti was considered a prophet by her fellow Pentecostal church members. Very hesitantly, she went to the Adventist church in Barasti for the first meeting in the NET series. After all, this is a church too, she rationalized.

The message pleased her, so she went to bed with a peaceful heart. However, during the night, the Lord came to her in a dream. "Why do you resist the good way to salvation?" He asked. "I want you to keep the Sabbath, as all entirely obedient children do."

Shocked, this woman awoke. Almost two years before, the Lord had revealed to her the seventh-day Sabbath and asked her to observe it. But in her zeal for the Pentecostal church, she had kept the revelation to herself. Now, she trembled as if it were the day of judgment.

On one of the following nights, she spoke in church, which she had done so many times before. This time, however, she no longer had the self-confidence of a prophet; she spoke with the broken heart of a sinner asking the Master to accept her as a submissive follower in the church of her dreams.

In the neighboring country of Moldova, a large group of people were gathered in a cemetery, where an Orthodox priest was conducting a funeral. Peter, a neighbor of the deceased, wasn't listening to the repetitive prayers. He was concerned about his wife, who, night after night, was attending the Adventist church for something they called "the NET."

Suddenly, he came back to reality, surprised by what the priest was doing. Rather than performing the funeral rites, he was threatening the people to keep them from going to the NET! "If I learn that you continue to go to the NET," he said, "you are dead meat! I will not christen your children. I will not receive you for confessional. I will deny you Communion! If one of you dies, let the dogs eat him—I will not perform his funeral!" And so on and so on. The poor people were listening like beaten penitents.

Then Peter exploded. "Father, enough is enough. Is this your task—to stop people from hearing the gospel? You would do better to stop the drunkards from going to the bars and the sinners from their cursed sins! Listen, Father, I haven't yet gone to the Adventists and the NET, but from now on, if you need me, you can find me there!" That night Peter and his wife were together in the church, with hearts open to learn the truth about God.

NET '98 influences world evangelism

God blessed NET '98 with more than twenty-five thousand baptisms, an electrified university campus, changed lives, renewed commitment, hearts mended, and a broadened vision. He performed miracles in unusual ways.

NET '98 was the fourth satellite NET evangelism series broadcast by the Adventist Church. It's the only satellite evangelistic series to date (2005) that's had the united participation of a global audience and the simultaneous translation and broadcast of forty languages. Some subsequent regional satellite NET events have had larger audiences than NET '98, and a number have had more baptisms, but none to date has had the global support or participation of this event.

The satellite uplink "dish farm" at Pioneer Memorial Church

Around the world, thousands of Seventh-day Adventists joined for five weeks to pray, fellowship, study, and witness together. Viewers focused on sharing God's love with their friends and neighbors, on finding and strengthening their relationship with their "forever Friend."

Both the presentations of Pastor Finley in the previous NET events of 1995 and 1996 and the presentations of Pastor Nelson in NET '98 led to a renewed confidence in the Adventist message. Many voices of dissent were stilled. Members developed a confidence in and identity with the world Adventist Church and its mission, which led to greater unity and greater understanding of the life and the growth to which God is calling us.

NET '98 was pivotal in the corporate church. Various regions of the world church accepted both the effectiveness of the satellite technology and the vital importance of contextualizing the broadcasts. It strongly stimulated the world church to begin equipping many local churches with downlink equipment, to develop media centers, and to foster regional NET programs and local NET speakers.

The Adventist Television Network began to experience its largest growth worldwide after this series. In 1998, the world church sponsored two satellite NET evangelistic programs; in the ensuing five years, fifty-nine were held (nine in 1999, twelve in 2000, eleven in 2001, twelve in 2002, and fifteen in 2003). Correspondingly, the number of churches equipped to receive satellite programs grew from approximately five thousand in 1998 to an estimated twenty thousand in 2005. Church TV media production centers increased from two in 1995 to forty in 2004. Increasingly, people began to call for direct-to-home, full-time Adventist television. This call culminated in the launch of the Hope Channels during the years 2002 to 2005.

To a large degree, NET '98 was also the catalyst for the use of Internet by the world Adventist Church. It opened new horizons, gave new tools, and broadened the communication and the spiritual world community of the Adventist Church. Digital technology in the Internet and DVDs has created a powerful synergy with video technology.

Pastor Alfred McClure, president of the North American Division of the Adventist Church at the time of NET '98, evaluated the series in these words: "The NeXt Millennium Seminar united the church in ways we've never seen before. And the unique thing was that around the world, Adventists and their guests heard the gospel presented in the same way."

Only eternity will reveal all the influence this unique and special satellite-evangelism series has had upon the church and upon individual lives.

Pastor Bullón

No extra technology. No graphics. Sermons no longer than thirty-five minutes. Evangelistic series no longer than ten days. Feature Bible stories. Make invitations every night. The preaching of Pastor Alejandro Bullón is so simple that you almost dismiss it. Yet Pastor Bullón is one of the most successful evangelists in the history of Adventism. The Holy Spirit has richly blessed his ministry.

Satellite evangelism is a thriving outreach in South America. Through it, Pastor Bullón and his team have seen nearly a half-million baptisms in cities scattered all over the Americas. (See appendix.) Born in the mountains of Peru of simple background, Pastor Bullón is perfectly bilingual in Spanish and Portuguese and speaks good English as well. His preaching is disarming, yet forceful. When you meet Pastor Bullón, you are impressed with his gentle, unpretentious spirit. The focus of his life and ministry is to help others come to know Jesus.

Every night, Pastor Bullón appeals to the hearts of his listeners to make decisions for Christ and truth. Every sermon appeal concludes with a song that fits his subject. As the appeal is being sung, Pastor Bullón always stands with a bowed head, praying for his audience to respond to the promptings of the Holy Spirit.

Arriving a day or two early in every city where he preaches, he mixes and mingles with the crowds. He sits quietly in cafés and walks the streets, all the time listening to people—listening to their stories. When he steps to the pulpit and preaches, he sprinkles his sermons with local illustrations. His audiences soon come to identify with him, which allows him to speak directly to their hearts. He teaches important Bible truths quietly and with humble simplicity, and when he appeals for his audience's decision to follow

Christ, they come forward with visible emotion. Surely, the Holy Spirit is present.

Pastor Bullón says the secret of his evangelistic success is based on a concept called "integrated evangelism." This concept, which the Adventist Church in South America

Pastor Bullón with two young Bolivians

promotes, envisions the church as a mighty team, every initiative of which leads to evangelism. Each member plays a vital role in using his or her gifts. "Our evangelism is based on months of preparation by our lay people and pastors," Pastor Bullón says. "Bible studies, small-group meetings, local seminars, evangelistic meetings—all [these] must precede [the satellite series] and be planned as follow-up." Pastor Bullón's role is to appeal for decision—to offer people an opportunity to follow the teachings they have learned and the convictions they have developed through months of preparation.

Pastor Bullón continues, "What is vitally important is the personal work of the members. In my preaching I can only assist what has already been sowed and then nurtured by the Holy Spirit. The members do what I can't do. I can't give thousands of Bible studies and visit thousands of interests. On the other hand, we professionals do what our members can't always do. On satellite, we can appeal for decisions and reach so many simultaneously with the opportunity of decision. The members can love and nurture the TV and satellite viewers into the church. This way we all work together, utilizing our spiritual gifts. And with God's blessing, thousands of earnest and prepared individuals are added to God's family."

Sonete Costa, who regularly sings the appeal songs for Pastor Bullón's evangelistic series, has experienced how powerful his sermons are. "So many times I have witnessed faces lit with the sweet peace of Heaven, faces painted with indescribable joy, and in contrast at times, the struggle with the powers of darkness as people wrestle to follow the promptings of the Holy Spirit. The Lord powerfully uses Pastor Bullón to reach people."

Each baptism is a testimony to the grace of Christ. Each conversion has a story. Here are just a few of Pastor Bullón's favorite stories of God's miraculous power to change lives.

United States, November 2002

"If you ever leave the house, I'll catch you and kill you!" shouted the angry husband to his wife. The little Mexican wife trembled; she knew his words were true. Her life with him was miserable. They fought all the time. He drank too much. He had many other women. He spent their money on his own interests. And many times he beat her unmercifully.

If I stay, he'll kill me, she thought. Maybe if I go far enough away, he won't ever find me. With this flicker of hope, she left her home. She hid during that day, and that night she crossed the river near their city and eventually made her way to the U.S. border. She crossed the border at night and began to walk in the desert. Fearing that the border patrol would catch her, she hid and slept during the day. For forty-five days, she continued her journey.

Eventually, the refugee reached California. She found a phone booth and called a cousin of hers who had left Mexico some years previously. This cousin picked her up and brought her to her home. She told the refugee that she was welcome to stay with her family. So, the refugee settled into the safety of her cousin's home.

Soon she discovered something that troubled her a great deal. When her cousin lived in Mexico, the two of them had shared a Roman Catholic heritage. Now, however, all her cousin's family had become Protestants, and they even went to church on Saturday. The refugee wasn't happy about this. She didn't like Protestants. One day she said, "I know I'm here with you, and you've been kind to me. But I wish you wouldn't speak to me anymore about the Bible or about Jesus Christ. Please stop."

Her cousin's family responded, "OK, we won't talk about these things that are disturbing to you—but on one condition. In fifteen days, our church will be part of a great event. Pastor Alejandro Bullón from South America will be preaching in Washington, D.C., and his meetings will be shown in our church. We want you to promise to come each night. If you promise this, we will not speak to you again about Jesus or the Bible."

The refugee agreed, and so it was that she went every night to the satellite-evangelism series. Each night she listened. She made no visible response to the calls to commitment, but the Holy Spirit was working on her heart.

One evening Pastor Bullón preached a powerful message on Lazarus. As he began his invitation, he said that if God's power was strong enough to raise the dead, surely He could restore dead marriages. This thought touched a tender chord in the refugee's heart.

Pastor Bullón continued by saying that God can't do anything for us unless we respond to His call. At this, the refugee stood up and made her way forward, joining many others standing at the front of the church. Tears ran down her face as her heart broke before God.

Suddenly, she felt a powerful grip on her arm. She turned—and nearly fainted. The person who had grasped her arm was her husband! He had promised to find her and kill her. Surely now she would die. How on earth had he found her here?

When she left her home in Mexico months before, he became completely enraged. He vowed to everyone that he would find his "terrible" wife and kill her as he had promised. He thought that maybe she had tried to escape to her cousin's home in the United States, so he headed there.

He made his way to the border, crossed it, and began the long journey through the desert, tracing her steps without even knowing it. Eventually, he too came to California. He had the address of her cousin's home, but of course, he would never call there.

Instead, when he found the home, he hid nearby, where he could watch it. Sure enough, he saw his wife there. She came and went—but was always with her cousin's family. She never traveled alone because she didn't know the city and was afraid.

The refugee's husband continued to stalk her, waiting for the time when she would be alone. He planned to kill her and then return to Mexico. No one would ever know what had happened.

When the satellite series began, he followed the family to the church and slipped into the back. Each night he listened to Pastor Bullón. Each night the Holy Spirit spoke to him. Each night his hard heart softened. When he saw his wife go forward, he too left his seat.

"Don't be afraid," he quietly whispered into her ear. "I too have been here every night this week, and I have given my heart to the Lord. I saw you make your decision tonight, and I wanted to come forward and join you."

Through God's miraculous providence, this couple was reunited and their dead marriage was resurrected. The refugee woman sensed her husband was a changed man. Two months later, the local pastor baptized them.

Argentina, August 1998

During the satellite series in Buenos Aires, Pastor Bullón preached on the subject of the Christian's responsibility. "Every Christian has to be personally responsible to Heaven for his or her actions," he said. Then, to illustrate his point, he told how much he loved his sons. "I don't know if my sons are watching me; they know I have dedicated my life to this ministry. When I die and am resurrected, my greatest joy will be to be united with my sons. Can you imagine my great suffering if even one is not in heaven with me?"

Later, an Adventist pastor told Pastor Bullón the most beautiful experience. Two of his sons had left the church many years before. Their choices had caused him and his wife great pain. The evening that Pastor Bullón used the illustration of his sons, this pastor's two sons, independent of each other, just happened to be in separate church downlink sites watching the sermon.

As Pastor Bullón told about his love for his sons, the two sons of this other pastor saw the face of their own father rather than that of Pastor Bullón. It was as if their father was expressing his great pain and his personal responsibility for his sons. Neither son could refuse the powerful call of the Holy Spirit that night. Independent of each other, they both decided to return to God and His church.

People fill a soccer stadium for Pastor Bullón's Peru series

Bolivia, September 2002

"Don't do this to me. You are really crazy!" Catherine's mother shouted at her in the stadium that Saturday morning. "How can you be so unhappy as to make such a ridiculous decision—deciding to be baptized? I don't like what you are doing. Why do you have to be so crazy?" People stared, but Catherine's mother continued her loud raving.

"Please, Mother, be quiet. Please don't speak to me like this in front of all these people!" pled Catherine.

On the other side of Catherine stood her friend and colleague, Harry, who had been raised a Seventh-day Adventist and who had introduced her to the Adventist Church. He was pressuring her too. "Everything is ready for the new TV show. All the choreography is done and the scores written for the musicians. Come with me—let's do the show together, and then later I will be baptized with you too."

At that very moment, Catherine's cell phone rang. It was someone from another TV station urging her to accept a very lucrative contract.

The angry voices and the pressure whirled around in Catherine's head. She looked up to the stage. Pastor Bullón called her name and invited her to come forward. Did she have the strength to go ahead with her decision to be baptized? As she stepped forward, Harry left in anger. Kind church brothers and sisters quieted her mother and surrounded Catherine as she walked toward Pastor Bullón.

Catherine Molina's story started many years before this first satellite series in Bolivia. She was an only child. She loved her parents, and they deeply loved her too. An ambitious girl, she had always wanted to be an actress, but her family disapproved. She loved music, but her parents didn't support the idea of music education either.

When she was in her late teens, she heard about a talent search in her home city of La Paz. She entered, and won third place. Not telling her family about her move into the world of music, she began to audition and sing at karaoke clubs. Doors opened wide, and soon she was recording her first CD. A second CD soon followed, and some of her songs hit number one in Bolivia. Plans began for a third CD and music videos. She became known throughout the country by her stage name, Taya.

Catherine's popularity as a singer led to a TV contract with Channel 7 in La Paz. Soon she had an invitation to host a variety show on Channel 21. She loved every minute of her work. As she hit the stage each weekend for her live show, the crew could hardly contain her. She danced, she sang, and she interviewed. Her success was mesmerizing.

During this time, she began a search for meaning and purpose. She became involved with the reading of tarot cards. She also connected with spiritualists, and strange things began to happen. She went almost two months without sleeping. Voices haunted her, and more than once she was awakened from fitful sleep by the sensation of hands encircling her throat and choking her.

Catherine's family became very concerned and took her to various doctors to find help. She tried different therapies. Sometimes she tried to avoid the people with the tarot cards, but they scared her by saying that her success had come through the devil, and if she left them, she would lose her popularity and all it had brought.

If there is a devil, then there must be a God, Catherine thought, so she began to try different churches. While visiting an evangelical church, she discovered for the first time the practice of reading the Bible. She went home with a Bible and tried several times to read it, opening it to various places, but it made no sense to her at first. Eventually, she turned to Genesis again, and this time, when she read "In the beginning, God . . . ," it was exactly what she needed to hear. Now she couldn't study the Bible enough.

About this time she met Harry, and they clicked immediately. He wanted to do a CD and a TV show with her, and he wanted to marry her. She laughed and said, "First, let's study the Bible."

"If you want to study the Bible, I know where you should go," Harry said. He'd grown up in an Adventist home but had left the church some time before. Despite his lack of interest in religion, he introduced Catherine to the Seventh-day Adventist Church. A young woman from one of the local churches offered to study the Bible with Catherine. She agreed, and they began studies immediately.

They studied together for hours—sometimes until eleven o'clock at night. Catherine soaked everything up like a dry sponge. The answers to her many questions brought a corresponding peace. Soon she knew that she wanted to be baptized.

Catherine attended the first meeting of the satellite series that was being broadcast from Cochabamba. At the end of the sermon, Pastor Bullón made a strong invitation. Catherine wanted to respond, but not in front of so many people, many of whom would recognize her. But she couldn't stay in her seat; she went forward in commitment, and in front of everyone cried like a baby. Then she felt an enormous sense of peace in her soul. Her search was over!

However, Catherine was still the host of a live TV show each Saturday night. That Saturday evening she went on stage to host her show. For the first time in her life, she didn't want to be there; it didn't feel right. Something inside her had changed. She didn't dance that night, and her manager and crew wondered if she was sick.

When Pastor Bullón returned to his hotel room after the conclusion of the satellite meeting that evening, he switched on the TV. To his shock, who should he see but Catherine, who had come forward and given her heart to Christ during his invitation. As he watched her, he felt a deep sadness. He thought that maybe her conversion wasn't genuine. He bowed his head and prayed for her.

Pastor Bullón didn't know it then, but that was Catherine's last show. The Holy Spirit was working in a dramatic way. Catherine longed to be baptized. She had discovered peace and hope in her life. She was determined not to turn back. She prayed that God would do three things for her. Each would be a miracle. Her first request was that she be freed from her TV and music contracts.

On Monday morning, she took all her dance costumes and dance CDs—and she had many!—to the TV station and told the management that she would no longer host her program. A very traumatic meeting ensued. The station management and producers were very upset. They loved her show. It was one of the most popular in Bolivia. She was supposed to release a brand-new music video in two weeks, and she was canceling everything! But they freed her of all obligations, and without penalty. That was one prayer answered. The other two were to follow later.

Meanwhile, Catherine continued to attend the downlink meetings in La Paz every evening. She wanted to be baptized, but was she ready? Even though she had studied for months, however, her Bible instructor was hesitant because Catherine was very secular in her appearance. And many questioned if her dramatic change was permanent. She still had things to learn.

One evening, Catherine became convicted about her jewelry. She said she was willing to take it off. The next morning, God helped her. Catherine had three rings in each ear. When she awoke that morning, she had a "mysterious" infection in her ears. She'd never had such an infection before. At that, she took off all her jewelry and never again put it back on.

During this time, Catherine's family was very upset and angry. They thought their star daughter had gone crazy. It was at this point that she convinced her mother to come to the Sabbath morning service in the stadium to hear Pastor Bullón, who was to preach in La Paz. During his invitation, when Catherine began to move forward in response, her mother erupted

Former Bolivian media star Catherine "Taya" Molina now sings for Christ

with shouts of dismay, Harry begged her not to go, and her cell phone rang with the unexpected offer of another lucrative TV contract. Talk about the great controversy being waged over a soul—this was a real battle! However, as Sonete Costa sang the appeal, Catherine came forward, determined to follow Jesus.

Catherine requested a private baptism. But when she met with Pastor Bullón, he explained the significance of baptism as a public testimony of one's commitment to Christ. Catherine was a national celebrity. Would a private baptism really witness to what Jesus was doing to change her life? No, Catherine decided. If she was going to be a Christian, then she wanted everyone to know. That Sabbath evening, she flew to Cochabamba and was part of the baptismal service broadcast via satellite. Her witness was electrifying.

A baptismal service during Pastor Bullón's Bolivian series

However, Catherine still had two unanswered prayers. Her second request was that God would provide religious books to satisfy her voracious appetite for reading. She wanted so badly to learn more of the teachings of the Bible and how to live the Christian life.

God answered this prayer by providing her with $600 that she could use to purchase books. And the same day that she received this money, a pastor gave her his entire library of books by Ellen G. White that covered Bible history. Catherine was thrilled with this second miracle!

Third, Catherine prayed that God would give her something to do for Him. She needed a job, and she wanted to minister for Jesus. The week she prayed about this desire, she received a call from the church headquarters in Bolivia asking her to come and work at the brand-new Bolivian Adventist media center.

Catherine works there today—a testimony to God's miraculous power to change lives. Once a popular TV star, she has traded worldly adulation for the quiet affirmation and peace of heaven.

Panama, April 1998

During a satellite series broadcast from Panama, Pastor Bullón preached about miracles. Maria,* a young woman originally from Colombia, had just come to Panama to find work. She was a nurse. Maria's neighbors were faithful Adventist lay people. Excited about the satellite meetings, they flooded her with invitations to come with them to hear the powerful messages. One evening she consented to go—basically, just to make them happy.

That evening, Pastor Bullón preached on the story of Mary, the prostitute. Maria's heart broke. She had failed to find a nursing position in Panama and had resorted to prostitution—selling her body to survive and to provide for her family, including a young son back home in Colombia. She abhorred her lifestyle, but felt there was no hope for her.

As Sonete Costa sang a beautiful appeal song about how God wants to give His children miracles from heaven, Maria's heart was touched. She believed in miracles. She went home that night and prayed that God would give her a miracle. Two days later, a wealthy woman called, asking Maria to work as a nanny in her home. Maria was thrilled—God had given her the miracle for which she had prayed. If God could do this, surely He could accept her as a sinful prostitute, as Pastor Bullón had preached. Maria began to study and eventually was baptized—another testimony to God's grace!

---

*Maria is not her real name.

ACTS 2000

Of the birth of the ACTS 2000 satellite-evangelism series, Pastor Mark Finley, speaker/director of the It Is Written (IIW) television ministry, says, "It happened after NET '96. I began to dream. I dreamed of a way—not to reach thousands, but hundreds of thousands, perhaps one million people, with the gospel. I dreamed of a way to make satellite evangelism more relevant to people in their diversified cultures and languages. The dream was to take satellite evangelism to several regions of the world with the stories, illustrations and graphics adapted to appeal to the people of each respective region." (*ACTS 2000 Remembered* souvenir edition.)

ACTS 2000 was the fulfillment of this dream. Envisioned and led by Pastor Finley and his wife, Ernestine, its impact on the world Adventist Church has been profound. Vital to its success was the strong support of IIW staff—particularly Pastor Royce Williams and Victor Pires—and the work of the Adventist Television Network (ATN) to put it on the air via satellite. The financial support of dedicated IIW partners made it all possible.

The name "ACTS 2000" is an acronym. "ACTS" comes from Adventist Communication Through Satellite. The "2000" refers to the millennium that began during this series. The name also refers to the biblical book of Acts and the miraculous outpouring of the Holy Spirit at Pentecost when the first millennium A.D. began. Just as Christianity spread worldwide at the beginning of the first millennium A.D., so ACTS 2000 was a series of ten large satellite NET events intended to invite as many people as possible worldwide to become part of the family of God at the beginning of the third millennium A.D.

Bucharest, Romania's Great Hall of the Palace during ACTS 2000

The satellite NET evangelism events that comprised ACTS 2000 definitely did have an impact on millions of people. The stories of the miracles that happened in the lives of people who experienced the fresh outpouring of God's Holy Spirit in this modern manifestation of Pentecost are far more exciting than uplink or downlink equipment issues, host venues, or committees and training classes. This chapter recounts some of the favorite experiences of Pastor Finley and the IIW team from the ACTS 2000 series and the many other satellite events they have conducted worldwide.

United States, October 1996

For years, Humberto Alvarez served as a judge in Communist Cuba. One day a Seventh-day Adventist pastor was brought before him, accused of sedition against the government. This pastor had been leading people to Jesus and selling Adventist literature. Judge Alvarez sentenced the pastor to three to five years in prison.

Some time later, Alvarez immigrated to Miami, Florida. But he had no job there, no vocation. One day when he was wandering, homeless and penniless on the streets, the son of an Adventist pastor invited him home for a meal. Alvarez enjoyed the excellent cooking of the pastor's wife and became a regular guest in the home. Eventually, he shared his background of being a former Cuban judge. His host said he knew an Adventist pastor who had lived in Cuba, and he arranged to introduce Alvarez to him. When they met, Alvarez was scared. He recognized the man as the pastor he had sentenced to prison years before. How would this man treat him now?

The Cuban pastor embraced Alvarez and assured him of his forgiveness and acceptance. The two men bonded immediately and began studying the Bible together. Weeks later, Alvarez attended the NET '96 satellite-evangelism meetings in Miami and made his decision for baptism.

Pastor Finley heard his story and invited Judge Alvarez to be baptized at the series host location in Orlando during a broadcast. These broadcasts covered all of North and South America and Europe. While Alvarez was in the baptismal pool, Pastor Finley interviewed him and the Cuban pastor. "Pastor, have you ever met this judge before?"

"Yes, I have."

"Where did you meet him?"

"In his courtroom."

"Where?"

"In Cuba."

"What did he say when you met him?"

"He condemned me."

"Judge, did you sentence this man to prison?"

"Yes."

"How long did you sentence him for?"

"Three to five years."

"Pastor, he sentenced you to prison; what are you going to do to him?"

'I'm going to baptize him and wash all his sins away.'

Thousands of miles away in Romania, another judge, Peter Molner, was watching the baptism taking place in Orlando. Judge Molner could hardly believe what he was seeing and hearing. He remembered the times during the Communist era when he had sent Adventist literature evangelists to prison. As he watched the baptism from Orlando, this Romanian judge made the decision to be baptized too.

Speaking of Romania, prior to NET '96, a dear woman in that country saved for five years to purchase a washing machine. When the members of her local Adventist church wanted to buy equipment so they could participate in the satellite series, a call was made for sacrificial offerings. This woman decided she could keep washing clothes for her family by hand on a wash-board. She cheerfully gave her painstakingly saved washing-machine money for the satellite equipment.

Another church member in Romania kept very busy driving visitors to and from the meetings. One day he found that he had no money to buy gas for his car. After the satellite meeting that evening, he was asked to take some people home. Going to his car, he found some money on the driver's seat. There was enough either to buy food for his family or to fill the tank. He used the money to buy gas. For the next three weeks, he drove the car—always filled with visitors—to and from the meetings. Throughout that time, the fuel gauge remained in the "full" position. Convinced that the gauge wasn't working, he went to the gas station to fill the tank. To his complete amazement and surprise, the gas tank actually was still full!

At many downlink sites in Europe, the growth in attendance during NET '96 was dramatic. While most people came to the meetings because of enthusiastic word-of-mouth invitations, at least one meeting had the ad-vantage of an unusual form of advertising. The mayor of a village in Tran-sylvania attended the first few meetings of the series. Then he commented to an Adventist church leader, "Your meetings are wonderful, but you peo-ple don't know how to advertise. You should have asked me, and I would have had the village drummer march through the village beating the drum and announcing the meetings."

"Would you still do that?" the Adventist asked.

"I surely will!" was his prompt reply. So each evening, the town drum-mer heralded the meetings, and attendance climbed dramatically. The meetings had become a village event.

The only location that church leaders in Madrid, Spain, could secure for a downlink site was a bar/theater. The first night, the 350 seats were filled to capacity, while the adjoining bar was nearly empty. "The people may not be drinking alcohol, but they are drinking in the Word of God!" someone observed. The second night, the local church leaders had to turn away four hundred people. The third night they made a videotape of the program and started double sessions.

Kustendil, a city in Bulgaria, was known for its crime, violence, and Mafia influence. Adventist church leaders there provided an outdoor screen, where a thousand people gathered each evening to take in Pastor Finley's sermons. City authorities actively encouraged people to attend, saying, "The more people who become Adventists, the less crime we will have in our town." (The preceding four stories appeared in It Is Written *Channels,* Fall/ Winter 1999.)

United States, 1998

It Is Written partners played a vital role in the support of the massive ACTS 2000 initiative. The following story, printed in IIW *Channels,* Fall/ Winter 1998, illustrates the sacrifice made by even the young to support this ministry.

My 10-year-old, Matthew, suffers from ADHD (attention deficit hyperactivity disorder). Yet we are astounded at God's mercy and grace in his life. We received a letter from you regarding ACTS 2000. Quite frankly, it sat on our table a few days, unopened, until it caught my son's attention, who, with normal childlike curiosity, said, "Dad, can I open it?"

"Sure!"

A few minutes later I noticed Matthew filling out the contribution card, and with normal adultlike curiosity, asked, "Hey, what are you doing?"

Matthew replied, "My friend Mark Finley needs some money to help reach those people, and God has touched my heart to help!"

On his own, moved by the Holy Spirit, Matthew had brought out all seven dollars he had stuffed in that funny-looking wallet with cartoon characters all over it. It was all the money he had earned last week from working in the farm area (voluntary, but they give the kids pocket change anyway). My son, plagued by this awful condition, still opened his heart to God's tender leading, to give all that he had. . . .

Moved to tears by my son's cheerful benevolence, I prayed with my wife, and we decided to multiply it and have included another $70 on top of his larger $7 contribution.

A postscript you will appreciate: On the outside of the envelope, he put his first name only. When I asked why he didn't include his last name, he said, "Because Pastor Finley knows who I am. He saw me at Arco Arena in Sacramento last year. He's my friend!"

Philippines, January 1999

Pastor Finley recounts in his own words a very special experience during ACTS 2000—Philippines in the city of Manila:

I was invited to go to the large, national prison called the Muntinglupa Prison. I was going to the prison for a baptism. Forty-seven prisoners wanted to be baptized, twenty-one of them from death row. We have an Adventist church in that prison which was established through twenty-two years of labor by a dedicated Adventist couple. Today there are 456 [Adventist church] members in that national prison. As I walked through the prison gates, our members put their arms around me and hugged me.

I walked down the narrow prison path to their little church. The prisoners came—tattooed men with scars on their faces. Many of them had committed the crimes of rape, robbery, aggravated assault, and murder. But there was something different about them. Their eyes now were sparkling. Their faces were shining. They didn't look like criminals. They were now my brothers in Christ.

I listened to a prison quartet sing, "Let's sing a happy song. Let's sing about Jesus. . . ."

As I listened to them sing, my heart was touched. Tears came to my eyes! I wept. Then I asked, "Who is the first tenor?"

"He's a former murderer."

"Who's the second tenor?"

"A former murderer."

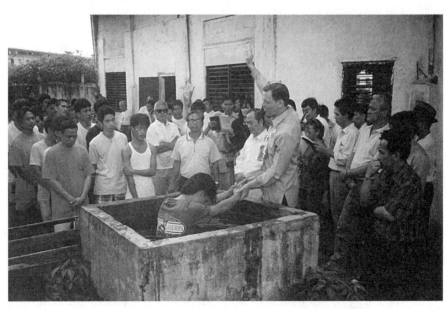

Pastor Mark Finley baptizes prisoners in the Philippines

"Who's the baritone?"

"He's a former murderer."

"Who's the bass?"

"A murderer."

A group of convicted murderers singing, "Let's sing a happy song! Let's sing about Jesus!"

Before I left that prison I made certain the pastor of the church would receive money to buy Bibles, a guitar so they could sing with it on death row, and money to buy the much-needed missionary supplies.

After the song service, I preached a sermon on God's forgiveness, grace, and power to change lives. And then we went outside for the baptism.

These prisoners had made a small baptistry. I had to stand outside of the baptistry. They stood inside. With one hand raised, my other hand on their head, I pushed them down under the water as they were baptized in the name of the Father, the Son, and the Holy Spirit. I hugged these prisoners. They were my brothers!

Chile, October 1999

On Silvia Tapia's first day as a volunteer telephone answerer for *Está Escrito,* the Spanish *It Is Written* television program in South America, the very first call she received was from an uncle she hadn't heard from in eighteen years. He had a problem with drugs, and in his search for God and for help to turn around, he had been watching *Está Escrito.* How surprised and thrilled Silvia was to be able to help her own uncle through prayer, Bible lessons, and the address of the church!

India, January 2000

India was the site of the sixth ACTS 2000 series. The Indian government concluded weeks of intense negotiations by denying a permit required to uplink the series. So the series began with Pastor Finley preaching an evangelistic campaign in Madras. These meetings were videotaped with simultaneous translation into eight major Indian languages. Then the videotapes were distributed throughout the country for evangelistic series in various locations.

During the baptism on the final day of the original series in the host location in Madras, an incident happened that vividly portrays the great-controversy battle over every person's decision. Pastor Finley stood on the

Women in India heading to a meeting

shore of a lake. As each group of baptismal candidates was immersed, he repeated the words, "I now baptize you in the name of the Father, Son, and Holy Spirit" (see Matthew 28:19, 20).

Suddenly, a wild shriek filled the air as a young woman ready to be immersed began screaming in the Tamil language, "Who are you? You must leave me!" Unseen hands pushed her under the water to drown her.

Nearby pastors grabbed her thrashing body and moved her toward shore. Breaking away, she lunged at Pastor Finley with fists flailing, screaming curses. Then she fell to the ground in violent contortions.

Along with the leader of the local Adventist churches and a group of pastors, Pastor Finley began praying earnestly for her deliverance. After a few minutes of intense struggle, she relaxed, and a look of sweet peace came over her face. She said, "Please, I want to be baptized now." Returning to the water, she was buried with Christ and came forth radiant and rejoicing. Another victory for the Lord Jesus Christ! (Adapted from *Channels,* Spring/Summer 2000.)

Brazil, June 2000

Pastor Royce Williams tells the following story: Friday, June 4, was Anna's birthday, and she felt that she had nothing for which to live. She sat down to write letters to her boyfriend, her parents, and even to God, telling them that she was going to end her life.

As she wrote, the telephone rang. She picked up the phone, and asked the caller, "Why are you calling me? I have a terrible, tragic thing to do. I'm going to commit suicide."

The caller, a deacon from the church at the Adventist college in Brazil, said, "I wasn't trying to call you; I happened to dial the wrong number. But I believe God led me to dial your number." Then he and Anna began to talk. They talked about life and eternity. They talked about forgiveness and mercy and God's love. And the deacon invited Anna to the evangelistic meetings that were being held in the college church.

Anna came to the meetings. When she heard the Word of God, she accepted Christ and gave her life to Him. As Pastor Finley made an altar call, she wept. With tears running down her face, she said, "Jesus, I am Yours! Jesus, I want to live! Jesus, give me a new purpose for living!"

Today she rejoices in following Jesus and the truths of the Bible that saved her life.

Jamaica, April 2001

The last Sabbath of this fourteen-day event was one of the most memorable ever for the It Is Written team. Long before the time for the morning service to begin in the national arena, members and visitors were claiming their seats. Eventually, seven thousand people crowded in to fill every seat and bleacher, and standing room was at a premium. The best Jamaican Adventist musicians provided the special music, and the congregational singing sent spiritual chills up one's spine.

The central focus Sabbath morning was a reserved section in front of the platform. There were baptismal candidates robed in brand-new gowns in the colors of the flag of Jamaica: some in green, some in gold, and some in black—perhaps the first time baptismal candidates have dressed in the colors of a nation's flag.

Pastor Finley taught a Bible class on how to live a victorious life in Jesus—a deeply spiritual presentation. After the worship service, Pastor Finley led a procession to the national swimming complex near the arena. Bleachers on each side of the pool allowed approximately three thousand people to view the service. A choir sang as the procession entered the complex, and forty-two pastors in black robes accented with the colors of the Jamaican flag were preparing to enter the pool. Some 395 baptismal candidates were seated in one set of bleachers, arranged in alternate rows of green, gold, and black, and ushers in red sashes occupied the top rows of the bleachers. What an impressive sight!

At the appointed moment, the forty-two pastors, each accompanied by a deacon, entered the pool, and the service began. When each successive set of candidates was in place, Pastor Finley spoke the words, "Now we pastors raise our hands to heaven and upon your acceptance of the Lord Jesus Christ as your personal Savior, we baptize you in the name of the Father, Son, and the Holy Spirit. Amen!" (Adapted from *Channels,* Fall/Winter 2001.)

Papua New Guinea, July 2001

Before the evangelistic team arrived, Papua New Guinea was in turmoil. There had been a long period of rising tension and significant civil disobedience. So, the government declared a state of emergency and imposed a curfew, which would have stopped the meetings. Miraculously, God opened the way for the meetings to begin.

The church in Papua New Guinea, with good reason, approached the opening night of July 6 with considerable concern. One week earlier, the Great Controversy was very evident in the unfolding of a drama in Port Moresby. University students began a peaceful demonstration against the proposed government land and business privatization plan. Things got out of hand, and the police reacted with gunfire. Four students died and many were wounded. Violence erupted in the streets, with looting and burning. A 7 P.M. to 5 A.M. curfew was imposed which would extend through July 10. The opening of the series was seriously threatened.

Email messages raced back and forth across the Pacific, with emergency committees meeting in the It Is Written office and in Port Moresby. Confident that God was still in control and would open a way, Pastor Finley and the team decided to move forward in faith.

[During ceremonies at the airport], Minister of Foreign Affairs John Pandari, a Seventh-day Adventist, gave a resounding welcome speech. He concluded with an announcement from the prime minister's office that the curfew would be adjusted to 12 midnight to 5 A.M. to allow the meetings to proceed as planned. You can imagine the roar of amens and shouting for joy over this good news. We praise God for this answer to prayer. It was a day none of us will forget.

The meetings were scheduled to begin on Friday, July 6. That day the national newspaper carried the following headline in very large letters: "CURFEW EASED FOR SDA RALLY." This was an answer to many days of earnest prayer not only throughout Papua New Guinea but also in other parts of the world. (*Channels,* Fall/Winter 2001.)

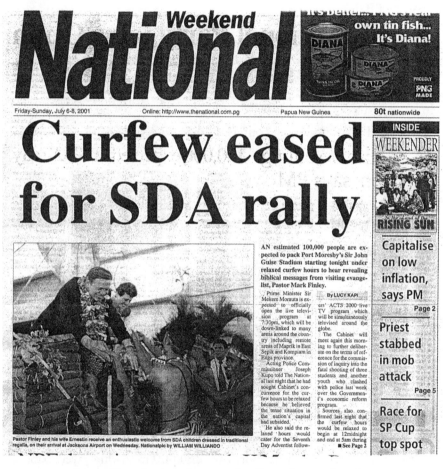

Papua New Guinea newspaper headlines change of curfew

The ACTS 2000—Papua New Guinea series had the largest crowds in the host venue of any satellite series to date. Nearly one hundred thousand people gathered in the Sir John Guise Stadium in Port Moresby each night. Nearly five hundred thousand more people participated at downlink sites scattered across Papua New Guinea. Additionally, many more listened on radio or watched the tape-delay series on national television.

The impact of ACTS 2000

ACTS 2000 motivated a tremendous expansion of the church-based satellite downlink network. Several key things happened that were significant for the church:

- Pastor Finley, the Adventist Church's first and most experienced satellite NET evangelistic speaker, brought his expertise to the participating regions of the world, establishing confidence in satellite NET evangelism.

- The ACTS 2000 series encouraged other Adventist entities and speakers to develop and conduct major satellite NET events.

- With every ACTS 2000 event, Pastor Finley conducted training programs for local pastors and key lay leaders. Significant amounts of evangelistic materials were provided to assist the local evangelistic initiatives. These events inspired key church and pastoral leadership regarding satellite NET evangelism and equipped them with new insights, skills, and materials to nurture and follow up these events.

- Combined with the previous NET events and other satellite broadcast events, the various ACTS 2000 series stimulated many thousands of local churches to invest in the equipment to broadcast and receive the programs. They also provided a huge stimulus for the expansion of the Adventist Television Network. In some cases, It Is Written and other entities and individuals provided subsidies to help churches to purchase equipment.

It Is Written reported that more than 150,000 individuals were baptized and became members of the Adventist Church through the ACTS 2000 series alone.

Section III:
Where it Happened

North America

"Do not despise this small beginning, for the eyes of the Lord rejoice to see the work begin" (Zechariah 4:10, TLB). The start of Adventist satellite broadcasting certainly fulfills the idea of "small beginnings"! The story of this small beginning is a modern thriller of the best kind—it tells how God used dedicated lay business people and visionary technical leaders to start a communication network that influences the lives of millions today.

United States, 1990

Pastor Robert Folkenberg and Pastor Al McClure were elected General Conference president and North American Division president during the 1990 General Conference session in Indianapolis. Soon after their election, Dan Houghton, president of Adventist Laymen's Services and Industries (ASI), asked them both, "What can ASI do to help you?" Their response came quickly: "If you can help us find a way to communicate more effectively with our churches, this would be a big help." Dan found this to be an interesting and challenging request.

In his infectiously enthusiastic style, Dan talked about the need and asked many people what they would do. When he posed the question to Warren Judd, vice president of the Adventist Media Center, Warren's response was decisive. "I would develop a church satellite network. Why not give the corporate church a way to talk simultaneously and directly to the members?"

Several months and many discussions later, ASI leaders decided to pursue the idea of a satellite network system. They asked Warren to give them a proposal on how the project could be developed. At this stage, they were thinking only of the North American Division, not the whole world.

Warren began to ponder the questions. What equipment was needed? How would it work? What would it cost? Would it be effective? Would the churches participate? He had noted the use of satellite broadcasts by the Mormon Church and had talked to many people in media circles about the viability of a church network system. Now he began in earnest to research equipment. He contacted numerous satellite receiver manufacturing companies.

In early 1991, many satellite receiver manufacturers sold only domestic receivers (IRDs) that limited viewers' access to channels. This was not ideal for the church application. We needed free-to-air (FTA) broadcast. Even more significantly, the technology was so complicated that most local churches would find it formidable.

Another serious challenge was the issue of satellite space. Leasing satellite time sporadically would be like trying to rent an apartment sporadically. There would be no guarantee that the church could obtain a channel on the same satellite or on the same frequency whenever it had something to broadcast. And the alternative—a couple thousand churches across the North American Division reaiming their antennas to a different satellite and tuning to new parameters and frequencies for each new broadcast—didn't seem practical. It seemed necessary to find equipment that could be automatically directed to the proper satellite and channel. However, equipment with this capability simply did not exist.

Encouraged by Pastor Phil Follett, a General Conference vice president, Warren consulted with Wilton Helm, an Adventist engineer. Wilton felt an existing receiver could be modified to do the task. A company named Chapparal sold a receiver for a business network that seemed to be suitable for such a modification. Wilton explained to the Chapparal engineers how he thought they could develop the technology, and, reluctantly, they agreed to go ahead. The design work was slow, tedious, and frustrating, and Warren and Wilton had to make multiple trips to San Jose, California, but eventually a working system was developed.

Then some in church leadership began to get cold feet; it seemed that few were enthusiastic about the project. But Warren wouldn't be deterred. He kept asking questions and gathering information. ASI leaders also continued to drive the project, insisting the church needed a feasible plan to develop a communication network. God was in the project, guiding Warren and others to persevere. Who would ever have guessed that a few years later the idea would catch on and wrap around the globe, catapulting the Adventist Church to the forefront in the use of cutting-edge technology to communicate the gospel?

United States, 1992

"Team, we're going to school this weekend. We're going to learn how to do live broadcast and uplink. The Adventist Church will be doing this, and we need to figure out how it's done. We are paying the people at HSN [Home Shopping Network] to teach us the ropes," Warren told his core group at Adventist Media Productions. They all thought Warren was crazy!

On his commute between Thousand Oaks and Loma Linda, California, Warren passed through the city of Ontario, where, near the freeway, the West Coast headquarters for HSN is located. One day Warren stopped in and talked about his dream of developing a church network. Then he asked if HSN would rent their studio and uplink for a couple hours when they weren't using it so he could test the idea with a live uplink to a few churches. It was an unusual request, but they graciously agreed.

In the meantime, Dan Houghton had been busy working with officers of the Southeastern California Conference to spearhead this totally new and innovative communication project for the church. The idea excited the conference leaders, and they bought into it. Five churches purchased the satellite reception equipment and had it installed.

Dan also worked with Pastor Mark Finley, who had recently been appointed as speaker of *It Is Written*. Dan decided the best way to start was for Pastor Finley to preach an inspirational message on the Second Coming. A date was set: November 21, 1992.

HSN had two large C-band uplink dishes, one for on-air broadcast and another for standby. They had a studio with cameras, could take phone calls on air, and had a crew accustomed to live broadcast production. Warren hired a director and a lighting director, rented metal bleachers, and booked the satellite time. Now the question was, Would the churches really receive this test broadcast?

So, that Sabbath afternoon a studio audience of about 150 gathered in the HSN studio. Dan Houghton's family provided a musical number, Pastor Finley preached a beautiful message on the Second Coming, and the members in the viewing audiences called in with questions and comments. The whole production and broadcast went off flawlessly, and the churches provided great feedback. Though it was a small beginning, Adventist Church communication via satellite was born!

On February 13, 1993, they did another test broadcast, again at the HSN studio. It was an identical setup, with Pastor Finley preaching and five churches downlinking the event. Once again, Warren took his technical team to learn everything they could about live production and uplink. And again, the results were excellent. Now the die was cast, and the Adventist Church in North America stepped out in a venture of faith to develop a church network.

Who could have imagined back then that someday Pastor Finley and others would preach in satellite NET events with thousands of downlinks and millions in the audience? How could Warren and his technical team— Colin Mead, Jerry Reed, and Randy Schornstein—have known that in the years to come, they would cross the globe numerous times with tons of equipment, producing and uplinking scores of live church events?

Russia, 1993

This is probably the most amazing and the stupidest thing I've ever done! Warren thought as he sat in an old video production truck in the center of Moscow, Russia, watching a program being captured live. Pastor Finley and his It Is Written team were finishing an evangelistic series in a sports stadium in Moscow. On the final Sabbath evening, the program was to be broadcast back to churches in North America, where members would be gathered Sabbath morning. By this time, approximately seventy churches had caught the vision, equipped themselves with satellite downlink equipment, and participated in some training events offered by the North American Division.

The denomination still had no uplink equipment of its own. On previous trips to Moscow, Warren had worked to locate production equipment he could use. He found that Russia's ZTV had a nice, old production truck built in Germany that he could rent for seventeen hundred dollars for the day, which was "insanely cheap" for a video production truck. Then he had to find a satellite that could be seen by an earth station on the East Coast of the United States.

Though from Moscow the Intelsat K satellite was very low on the horizon, an earth station in Virginia could pick up its signal and relay it to a satellite over North America, from which the churches could access the program. But how could they get the signal from the sports stadium to ZTV in downtown Moscow? Warren discovered that the Bright Star company had a channel used for backhauling Reuters news service to New York. They were connected by cable to a hub in Moscow.

However, there were obstacles. On the day of the broadcast, while the It Is Written team was using half of the state-owned stadium, a rock concert was taking place in the other half. A divider of sorts made of supposedly soundproof material ran down the center of the stadium. Worse, the government was threatening to close down the Adventist program. It looked like the final meeting would not happen, let alone be broadcast back to the United States. The Adventist team prayed fervently for Heaven to intervene so Pastor Finley could conclude the series and the live broadcast could take place.

ZTV came that Sabbath with their production truck and two huge lights on stands. Warren just groaned. Oh no! he thought. We can't possibly light the stage and Pastor Finley properly for broadcast with only two lights. Nevertheless, the production proceeded. Warren remembers, "I sat in the production truck, and the pictures in the truck were bad. The cameras were poorly adjusted, and quite frankly, it was a wonder it happened. Everything you shouldn't do in production was done that day!"

During the sermon, a mentally unbalanced woman rushed to the platform and wrestled the mike away from Pastor Finley. Somehow, this drama wasn't clearly visible to the viewing audience in the United States, but it added to the excitement of the first Adventist international broadcast.

When Pastor Finley's sermon and the broadcast ended as scheduled, the earth station in Virginia immediately switched to their regular programming. People sitting spellbound in Adventist churches bowed their heads as Pastor Finley prayed. When they opened their eyes, they were shocked to see horses charging around a track in the middle of a race—not exactly appropriate for church viewing! Nevertheless, it was a historic moment in the life of the Adventist Church, as the first successful international live broadcast ended. After this experience, the technical team always purchased enough satellite time to ensure that the horse race gaffe never happened again!

Brazil, 1993

Shortly after the success in Moscow, the Voice of Prophecy was celebrating fifty years of ministry in Brazil with a three-week tour through that country. Pastor H. M. S. Richards, Jr., and his team were to visit many locations, finishing at a stadium with a capacity of twelve or fifteen thousand in the large city of São Paulo. With a growing network of downlink-equipped churches back in the United States, the Voice of Prophecy wanted to share the Brazilian celebration with supporters back home via satellite in a live uplink.

"Pastor, will you come to Brazil and translate for me?" Warren asked Pastor Henry Feyerabend, the founder of the Brazilian Voice of Prophecy.

He gladly consented. Having ministered for years in Brazil, he spoke Portuguese fluently and was eager to visit Brazil again. Warren knew no one in the broadcast industry in Brazil, had no leads, and had only Pastor Feyerabend to help him. They sat together in the Voice of Prophecy office armed with a phone book and began calling one production company after another. They talked to all sorts of companies before they finally found one that had a small production flight pack. It was simple equipment, but it would do the job. Warren contracted for their services.

Then Warren put together a production team of Brazilian Adventists, including Jonatan Conceirçao and Tennison Shirai, for a whirlwind tour with *Voice of Prophecy.* They captured as much as possible on a camera in Hi-8 video. The video editor couldn't speak a word of English, but Warren sat with her to edit a fifteen-minute documentary piece about the .tour, which would be shown during the final program in São Paulo.

The stadium where the final program was to be conducted had no uplink equipment—no cables, no wires, nothing to deliver the signal to Embratel, the company with which Warren contracted to uplink the program back to the earth station in Virginia. Embratel's uplink location was ten miles or so from the stadium.

Warren spent days working on a solution. Finally, someone told him about Francisco, who owned a freelance microwave business. When Warren contacted him and explained what he needed, Francisco confidently said, "No problem. We can do this—it's quite easy."

On the Sabbath of the live broadcast, Francisco showed up with a small microwave dish, which he attached with something like duct tape to a balcony at the stadium. "It works," he said. "We're ready." Warren thought to himself, *Yeah, right!*

Francisco quieted Warren's skepticism by a simple "I've tested it, and Embratel is receiving my signal. It will work for you."

However, entrusting an international broadcast to a small microwave dish mounted with duct tape strained Warren's nerves!

Communication was another problem—or three of them. Warren had to work with the Brazilian production team through a translator. He had to use an old, heavy, analogue cell phone to speak with Colin Mead at the earth station in Virginia. And all the while, he was trying to communicate with the American Voice of Prophecy team, which had assembled backstage and was ready to begin the program. "When you think about it all, it was really incredibly ambitious to take on what we did. Broadcasting international events—it was crazy! We didn't know anything," Warren recalls.

Despite the lack of experience, the Lord was behind the project, and another successful broadcast took place—with only one small hitch. Two minutes before the scheduled start that Sabbath afternoon, church members sat watching and waiting at downlinks across North America. Then they heard the nervous voice of dear Pastor H. M. S. Richards, Jr., backstage in São Paulo anxiously admonishing his team, "Hurry up! Come on! Let's go! Let's go!" Pastor Richards's lapel mike was on, and Warren had no way to tell the production team to turn off the audio. The angels must have smiled that evening as they applauded the second international live broadcast of the world Seventh-day Adventist Church.

Considering subsequent technological developments and the current broadcasting capabilities of Adventist Television Network, this was a very small beginning. We might be tempted to laugh when we see it in contrast to the equipment that the Adventist Television Network has now and the transcontinental broadcasts that it does every day. However, this small, inauspicious beginning was a bold step. Funds were scarce. And there was no road map. No "ten-year development plan." No clear consensus on programming. There was only a vision and a willingness to step out in faith and see what God would do. He opened the doors step by step. Thank God for small beginnings!

Today, ATN faces equally large challenges. What is happening currently with the ATN Hope Channels is likewise small and inauspicious. In contrast to the Goliaths of the world's communication industry that pour out their slick, skeptical, materialistic propaganda, the Hope channels may appear to be puny pebbles in the hand of the simple shepherd boy David. The only reasonable explanation for ATN's success despite a lack of knowledge and experience is best summarized in the words that Stanley Ponniah quoted: " 'God doesn't call the qualified; God qualifies the called.' "

In faith, the world church can go forward, knowing that God will continue to bless and provide just as He has in the past. This method of witness may seem small and insignificant today, but with God's blessing and the church's support, it will continue to grow and to reach millions with the message of Jesus' soon return.

Europe

NET '95 created a buzz throughout the worldwide Adventist family: The technology worked. Churches could equip themselves and receive the programs relatively easily. Satellite evangelism was productive—with only 676 sites participating, more than seven thousand people had been baptized. It was cost effective. This amazing technology shared the gifts of one evangelist in hundreds of locations.

Now the question was, Would satellite evangelism work in other countries and through multiple translations? Would it work in secular cultures outside North America? Many openly said it wouldn't.

Pastor Brad Thorp had served as the coordinator of NET '95, particularly for the host location, Chattanooga, Tennessee. Although originally from Canada, he was employed by the church in central Europe as associate ministerial secretary and director of the Mobile Church-Growth and Evangelism Institute. By 1995, he (and our family) had traveled throughout Europe for nine years, training pastors in evangelism and church growth. Hundreds of pastors had attended these institutes and learned principles of church growth and how to conduct successful evangelistic series. These principles were the same ones at the foundation of the early satellite-evangelism events.

When Brad returned to his responsibilities in Europe after NET '95, he told others how well the program had worked. Pastor Robert Folkenberg, then General Conference president, encouraged leaders in Europe to consider using satellite evangelism. Naturally, there were reservations:

- Evangelism in North America is much easier than secular Europe. Wouldn't that be just as true of satellite evangelism?

- Could satellite evangelism work through simultaneous translation?
- How would Europeans, who are more reserved than Americans are, respond to an American approach in evangelism?
- Was it technically possible to broadcast multiple languages to a different continent?

These were only a few of the questions that confronted church members and leaders as they carefully evaluated whether satellite evangelism could jump the barriers of oceans, continents, cultures, and languages for NET '96. The following stories reveal some of the ways God guided in establishing satellite evangelism in Europe.

Europe, November 1995

"Brother Thorp, NET '95 was an interesting program for the Americans, but satellite evangelism is not for Europe." "Europeans won't respond to an American speaker through translation." "NET '96 won't work for Europe." Many lay and church leaders voiced these and similar sentiments. Nevertheless, church leadership in central Europe invited Brad to share a report of NET '95 during their year-end planning meetings. After the inspiring report, various delegates began to ask questions, and a lively discussion followed.

Brother Makowski, president of the large, denominationally owned DE-VAU-GE Food factory in Germany, analyzed the costs and benefits and expressed his strong support. Pastor Rupp of the church in north Germany expressed his desire for the churches in his region to share in NET '96. Some others also saw the potential and thought they should explore the concept.

With the strong support of Pastor Frikart and Pastor Amelung, president and executive treasurer of the Euro-Africa Division, and many other leaders, it was voted to proceed. NET '96 would come to Europe.

Germany, February 1996

There was so much that had to be done—and in a culture where people cautiously analyze opportunities well ahead of time, carefully plan their actions, and then vigilantly execute them. Church leaders in north Germany voted for Pastor Matthias Mueller to be the German NET '96 coordinator.

Brad and Pastor Mueller pondered what would be a reasonable goal by which to evaluate success. After consulting with other leaders in Germany,

Pastor Mueller said that a reasonable goal for the German churches would be to have an average of one to two baptisms per church. In the very secular environment of central Europe, this would be considered a success.

Time was of the essence, and there wasn't much time to bring the German churches on board. Establishing efficient communication posed a big challenge. Matthias urged the leaders and pastors to get on CompuServe. Email was quite new, but Matthias was convinced it offered the only possibility of communicating information with the dispatch that would be needed if this new outreach project to the German-speaking churches were to work.

There was the challenge of obtaining satellite equipment. In North America, the churches had installed large, C-band dish antennas that receive analogue broadcasts. In Europe's crowded cites, churches wouldn't be able to use these large dishes; they'd have to use the smaller, digital, Ku-band dishes. That meant they also had to obtain free-to-air, "open" digital systems.

Stefan Fraunberger, engineer for *Stimme der Hoffnung* ("Voice of Hope," the German equivalent of the *Voice of Prophecy*), began to search for a supplier for small dishes. Three Angels Broadcasting Network (3ABN) was supplying the broadcast and had a source for the receivers. And Ernst Seegler owned an audio-visual company in Germany; he graciously offered the churches an excellent price on video projectors.

The German churches ordered the other equipment through Stimme der Hoffnung, which sent Agnus Proksch throughout Germany to deliver and install the dishes. During the time Agnus was doing this, he had two vehicular accidents. While driving his own vehicle, he was rear-ended. He then rented a van—and, while it was loaded with equipment, he had another accident in which the van was totaled. Miraculously, nothing was damaged. These accidents seemed more than coincidental. Agnus is a very careful person and had never before been involved in an auto accident. Despite the accidents, he went on to assist some of the 141 churches in Germany that installed equipment.

The churches in Germany weren't the only ones in central Europe that were preparing. Church leaders from Portugal, Spain, Austria, Switzerland, the Czech Republic, and Slovakia didn't want their countries to be left out, and they launched into this adventure. Early in September, Brad crisscrossed Europe, visiting many of these countries and meeting with groups of pastors and leaders to provide training.

In the northern areas of Europe, Pastor Miroslav Pujic reported in an email: "This is a very special day for me. You can't imagine how I am excited and thankful to the Lord. [We have] reached the number of 300 churches. It wasn't easy, but joyful. Thanks a lot for your support."

Churches in England, Norway, Netherlands, Hungary, Croatia, and Yugoslavia along with seven in the Baltic region also prepared for NET '96. A Canadian donor made it possible for fifty churches in Poland to participate.

Romania, 1996

When Brad was conducting an evangelistic series in Arad, Romania, Pastor Adrian Bocaneanu, president of the church in that country, expressed his interest in Romania's being part of the new satellite-evangelism venture. "Adrian," Brad replied, "although I think satellite evangelism has tremendous possibilities for the church, frankly, I don't think it is right for Romania. The equipment is just too expensive for the church members." This was shortly after Communism had fallen in that country. The economy was very poor, and inflation was rampant. To equip a church in Romania with the necessary equipment would cost the equivalent of twenty-seven months of the average church member's salary. Brad believed this was too high a price to pay.

A baptism in Romania resulting from ACTS 2000

Nevertheless, during a meeting in February 1996, Brad shared with the pastors the story of NET '95. He did so, he said, not because he thought they should be involved now, but in the hope that someday, satellite evangelism would reach Romania too.

However, the pastors began to discuss the concept. Why couldn't Romania get involved? Maybe obtaining this new technology for evangelism wasn't so impossible. What exactly did the equipment cost? News quickly spread by word of mouth, and churches began to make a commitment to raise the funds to participate.

"Brother Thorp," someone asked, "when do we have to pay for the special equipment?" "What do you mean?" Brad responded. The answer surprised him: "We need time to grow and sell our tomato crops."

The orders and money for the equipment started to arrive: eight, forty, one hundred—and still more orders came. No one could believe it! A few months later, Pastor Bocaneanu reported in an email:

> The latest count of Romanian churches to participate in NET '96 is 371. Most of them are buying the complete package. . . . I am still unable to believe that this is a reality and not a wild dream. I am totally amazed and humbled by the evangelistic vision and the sacrificial generosity of our members. In many places all the money for the equipment was raised in just one Sabbath. In one place, when they totaled the money they have received, it was found to be an excess of about one-third. They went to the church and said that they don't expect anybody to reclaim this excess, but that they would rather raise the balance to buy the equipment for a new church, a daughter church. And this is what they've done. . . . It is good to keep in mind that the average monthly wage is $50–$60 and that a sizable portion of our church is made up of young students, women who are alone in the church, and many of our churches are involved in a building program.

Romania proved to be exceptionally challenging in another way: The customs people posed many problems because of all the equipment shipped in. But the churches worked frantically right up to the last moment. Their effort was definitely worthwhile—in Romania, the nightly audience for NET '96 ranged between sixty and eighty thousand viewers!

Brad says his experience in Romania taught him a tremendous lesson. If it had been left up to him, Romania would not have participated; he thought the price was too high. But God showed him the power of His Spirit in leading our brothers and sisters to sacrifice for His work. They put in long days at the hard work of growing tomatoes commercially. This experience both humbled and inspired us; we've told this story of faith and sacrifice hundreds of times around the world.

Portugal, July 1996

Pastor Joaquim Dias, president of the Adventist Church in Portugal, emailed: "It is wonderful [how] our people are supporting NET '96 campaign. I am very pleased to inform you that, so far, 64 churches in Portugal are being equipped to have NET '96. . . . The printing material is being prepared by our publishing house. . . . Now we want to concentrate our efforts in getting people involved in Bible studies and in looking for the former church members."

In just a few short months, what had seemed impossible had been accomplished. More than a thousand sites across Europe were preparing for NET '96. No one had guessed church members and leaders would have this degree of interest.

The *Adventist Review* of February 1997 featured an article with stories about NET '96. The article included the following quote from a letter that Pastor Ulrich Frikart wrote to Pastor Al McClure, president of the North American Division:

> "Seven hundred and fifty churches prepared for NET '96, an evangelistic thrust without precedent in our division. A genuine miracle! An American evangelist was enthusiastically listened to in Europe! Seven thousand five hundred people responded to the call for baptism; 2000 of them have already been baptized. Small churches are coming back to life and growth."

Amazingly, some months later when the German baptismal statistics were tallied, they showed that the churches averaged four or five baptisms apiece. This was more than double what Brad and Pastor Mueller set as their measure of success. It was an extraordinary result in a region where growing the church has been very challenging.

Especially in Europe, NET '96 was a miraculous, providential act of God. Jumping the barriers of oceans, continents, nations, cultures, languages, finance, and history, Pastor Finley's prophetic preaching provided dramatic evidence that it is the power of the gospel that wins hearts. It showed that Adventists are bound together by their common understanding of the Bible and their mission to prepare people for the second coming of Jesus. A stronger sense of unity, identity, and belonging developed.

Today, Adventist Television Network continues to expand rapidly in Europe. When Hope Channel began, Pastors Bertil Wiklander and Miroslav Pujic, from the Trans-European Division headquarters, pressed us to make Hope Channel available on the Hotbird direct-to-home network. The European church members sacrificed financially to make this possible.

We launched Hope Channel—Europe in the middle of 2005. This, the sixth of the Hope Channel networks, provides opportunity for blocks of European language program-

Temporary uplink site near Collonges, France, for ATN broadcasts to Europe and Africa

ming, along with English programming. Adventist Television Network has specifically designed this channel to facilitate the contextualization of the Adventist message to the European culture. This channel also provides to the expanding church media centers of Europe the opportunity to broadcast to their constituencies as well as to evangelistic audiences. Today, via Hotbird, Hope Channel is available to more than 110 million homes stretching from the north of Europe to the northern Sahara, and from Portugal to the Caucasus Mountains in Russia. It covers the Middle East to the middle of Afghanistan.

Germany and Romania are currently building large media centers that will allow expanded media ministry. The church has secured cable and rebroadcast licenses for Hope Channel—Europe in some countries and has applied for them in others.

South America

Every five years, the Seventh-day Adventist Church conducts a business meeting attended by delegates from around the world—the General Conference session. This is a high point in Adventist Church life. In 1995, this world convention took place in Utrecht, Holland. Pastor Erlo Braun planned to prepare a video report of this event, which he would then broadcast in Brazil. Then, providentially, the opportunity developed for him to do a live, three-hour satellite broadcast direct from Utrecht. God used this circumstance to launch satellite TV ministry for all of South America—plus full-time Hope Channels in both Portuguese and Spanish that now bring the gospel to millions every day!

Pastor Braun was the director of the Brazilian It Is Written (IIW) ministry. A few months before the General Conference session, he had been working on a project. It Is Written wanted to be able to offer gifts to their viewers, and he needed a telephone system with an 800 number that viewers could call for free in response to these offers. So Pastor Braun visited the Rio de Janeiro offices of Embratel, the telecommunication authority of the Brazilian government.

During a tour of the facilities, he learned that Embratel had live broadcast capabilities. In fact, the Brazilian government owned auditoriums in fifty or sixty locations, including all the state capitals and major cities across Brazil. Embratel could broadcast a live program to all these venues.

Hmm . . . interesting! Immediately, Pastor Braun thought of the upcoming General Conference session. He asked, "Can we rent this network?" When he received an affirmative answer, in faith, he made a reservation for July and then began to work in earnest to bring to church members in Brazil a video report on the General Conference session produced by the IIW team—something that had never before been possible. Then Pastor Braun added to the program a three-hour live broadcast directly from Utrecht.

The 1995 General Conference session

As word spread throughout the Brazilian Adventist churches, members became excited. The larger Embratel auditoriums seated around two hundred, and the smaller rooms, only thirty to forty. Soon it became obvious that the Embratel venues would be too small. So, Pastor Braun encouraged the members to put up antenna dishes on their churches.

IIW sent a team of five to Utrecht: Pastor Braun, Jonatan Conceição, Pastor Williams Costa, Jr., and his wife, Sonete, along with Alexandre "Sacha" Ostrowski. With their one Betacam camera, they worked hard gathering interviews, reports, and footage from the convention floor. Before the final weekend of the session, some of the team flew back home to Rio de Janeiro and, with limited gear, worked forty-eight hours straight editing their video report. "We worked around the clock. We never slept!" Marcelo Vallado laughs and shakes his head.

Could they pull it all off? In spite of all the difficulties, the live program, including the segment from Utrecht, went very well. The Brazilian Adventists loved it. They filled fifty-six Embratel locations plus seventy-five Adventist churches that had installed big, C-band satellite dishes to receive the program. Pastor Braun and his team were exhausted but ecstatic. This was a new day in South America!

What about the future? Could the church use this technology for evangelism and for nurturing members? The team thought about the possibility of uplinking monthly programs, as Adventist Communication Network was doing in North America. Then they heard about NET '96 and decided that program was worth exploring. Pastor Braun flew to the United States and participated in a pastors' training course with Pastor Finley. Believing the church in Brazil would be interested in NET '96, Pastor Braun and the team once again stepped out in faith. At the same time, they started pursuing TV distribution options for the IIW ministry.

For some time, IIW had been airing weekly telecasts in Brazil. It was very expensive, costing ten thousand dollars each Sunday for a half-hour program. Brazilian ASI business people were sponsoring this weekly telecast. They encouraged Pastor Braun to try to get IIW programs broadcast to a much larger public audience by obtaining a daily half-hour program slot.

Pastor Braun and an influential businessperson, Dr. João Apolinário, met with management personnel at SBT, the second largest TV channel in Brazil. The meeting was discouraging. In the first place, all the time slots were full. Second, if a slot were available, it would cost more than four hundred thousand dollars a month just for the half-hour daily program!

When the meeting ended and Pastor Braun and Dr. Apolinário were leaving, SBT's program director, Mr. Stoliar, stopped the group. He said that an Adventist grandmother had raised him. "I like the Seventh-day Adventist Church. When I was a little boy, I used to sing in the choir at an Adventist school," he continued. "SBT is impossible, but why don't you think about some other possibilities for gaining a larger viewing audience for your program?" Then he suggested that they look into the new low-power television technology.

Immediately, Pastor Braun started to dream. Could they open a low-power TV station?

April 1996

Pastor Braun went back to Embratel, the sole telecommunications agent for Brazil, and asked permission to start a low-power TV station. The personnel laughed at him. "Impossible! You'll never get broadcast permission or satellite space."

But Pastor Braun wouldn't be deterred; he needed an immediate solution so he could broadcast NET '96. He decided that he would go directly to the national government in Brasilia and make a personal appeal on behalf of the Adventist Church.

Just before the start of his appointment with the minister of communication, someone at Embratel called Pastor Braun. "Erlo," he said, "a miracle has happened. Don't bother talking to the minister. Come back immediately. We have a great deal for you; we know a company that can put it all together. And space has just become available on an Intelsat satellite—you can have a channel!"

The Brazilian government had just agreed to allow Embratel to resell international channels on Intelsat satellites to private companies in Brazil. A company had backed out of a long-term agreement, and Embratel was eager to find another client to fill that segment.

Pastor Braun couldn't believe it. A channel was available? What did God have in mind? He was looking for only a half-hour daily segment and space for NET '96. How on earth could the church buy and use a full-time channel?

Then he thought, *Wait a minute! The church really did need a full-time channel. How much better this would be than just a single Sunday morning telecast. This was also the solution for broadcasting NET '96.* So, Pastor Braun decided that he would pursue this idea some more.

Providentially, another piece of the puzzle fell into place at this time. Philanthropist Dr. Milton Afonso, founder of Golden Cross Insurance Company in Brazil, was visiting with Pastor Folkenberg in Russia. He shared with him how he had recently observed the birth of a new religious TV channel in Brazil. A Pentecostal pastor had started it and had begun full-time broadcasting. In a short time, this channel became really popular in Brazil.

Dr. Afonso has a passion for the outreach of his church, particularly through communication media. He was quite frustrated that another denomination had so quickly established such a large TV presence. He too had begun to dream of the Adventist Church having a full-time channel. "Why should another church be doing something the Adventist Church could do? If the Pentecostals can do this, so can the Adventists!" Pastor Folkenberg encouraged Dr. Afonso to fund a TV ministry for the South America church using the brand-new technology that significantly reduced satellite costs.

Without knowing of Pastor Folkenberg's suggestion, Pastor Braun set up an appointment with Dr. Afonso when he returned from Russia. Pastor Braun shared with him the opportunity Embratel was presenting for a full-time broadcast. "Dr Afonso, with a full-time channel, we don't have to worry about broadcasting *It Is Written* once a week. We can broadcast it several times a day!"

Dr. Afonso listened carefully and then said, "Let's do it!"

Pastor Braun couldn't believe it. He hadn't expected Dr. Afonso to agree so quickly to such a bold plan. It was a miracle!

So, Golden Cross signed a ten-year contract with Embratel for use of the I-709 satellite. Now the church had a channel. The upcoming NET '96 would be an excellent opportunity for more churches to get involved.

However, they faced a very serious problem. The contract with Intelsat was based on a new, digital standard. Unfortunately, the seventy-five churches across Brazil that had purchased equipment a few months earlier to receive the broadcast from the General Conference session had installed analogue equipment. If the South American church were to move ahead with full-time TV ministry, the local congregations would have to replace the still-new equipment that they had just installed. Understandably, the church members thought this was crazy, and they were upset. They'd purchased equipment, used it only once, and now it was no good?

During this time, Dr. Afonso gave tremendous encouragement and support to this new project. With undimmed vision and zeal for proclaiming our message through TV, he donated to the church a former Golden Cross employee-training center in Novo Friburgo, near Rio de Janeiro, to become a TV media production center for Brazil. He also provided a complete production suite of equipment, a mobile uplink truck, and permanent uplink equipment. And he was so eager to see this new communication system up and running that he subsidized churches' purchase of the new downlink equipment. Only Heaven's prompting could have moved Dr. Afonso to do all this.

Then other problems arose: obtaining equipment, getting it through customs, shipping, and distribution. It seemed that in every direction they turned, they encountered more obstacles. Less than a month before the start of NET '96, they didn't have downlink equipment in the churches. However, praying earnestly and with determination, Pastor Braun's team overcame these tremendous difficulties. Miraculously, when NET '96 started, 350 churches were equipped and ready for satellite evangelism.

NET '96

NET '96 was a wonderful blessing. The 350 churches were open night after night, receiving the broadcast and presenting the powerful preaching of Pastor Finley. Everyone was thrilled with the clear digital broadcasts. The Brazilians appreciated being able to see and to hear in Portuguese a program that united them with the North American church.

One night an unexpected problem developed that became rather amusing. To make the programs attractive to the Brazilian audience, the person who provided the "voice" used for Pastor Finley's Brazilian *It Is Written* programs lip-synched each sermon in Portuguese. Unfortunately, this person developed laryngitis, and for several evenings, Pastor Finley's "voice" was hoarse!

When NET '96 was over, the Brazilian media team began uplinking a daily six-hour broadcast. Jonatan Conceição, media center head of production, was in charge of scheduling and programming. Starting the full-time channel was a bigger job than anticipated. There were many growing pains. "We dealt with a hundred different problems on a daily basis," Marcelo Vallado, media center operations manager at that time, remembers. "It was tough. We had major TV and radio construction projects going on, with studios, editing bays, et cetera, and in addition to all of that, the normal weekly work load for the *Voice of Prophecy, It Is Written,* and other ministries that never went away."

The technical crew, celebrating the first transmission (1996)

The church in Brazil hadn't used satellite evangelism before. It had no network for promoting the channel. Misunderstandings about the digital technology arose. And they were able to get only a few programs on public networks. So, naturally, many questioned the value of the heavy investment. How could the church properly manage this valuable resource and maximize its potential? How could church organizations share the operating costs effectively?

Despite all these challenges, church leadership recognized that digital communication was the way of the future, and they were willing to look for a solution. Dr. Afonso continued to give dedicated support. The Adventist world Church leadership, including Pastor Robert Folkenberg and Pastor Phil Follett, strongly supported the development of the South American TV ministry, as did the South American Division leadership, including Pastor Marino Oliveira and Pastor Ruy Nagel.

And God was in control. Gradually, He opened doors and provided solutions. The South American Division moved all its radio and Bible school operations to Novo Friburgo. This gave greater economy of scale to the operation. The General Conference assisted with the satellite and uplink operations. More staff joined the team.

"Everything that we have done here in the past eight years is a miracle," says Jorge Florencio. He's the uplink engineer for the full-time Portuguese and Spanish TV Hope channels. He never imagined being involved in TV uplink work. In fact, a few years earlier, doctors had told him he wouldn't probably live much longer because he had tuberculosis and 75 percent of his lungs was lost. It took him months to recover from his illness. As he lay confined to his bed, he kept asking God, "What should I do with my life?"

When Jorge joined the TV team in 1995, he didn't know anything about TV uplink and broadcast. He was very young, just barely out of academy, and was volunteering as an intern to learn what he could. He didn't believe people would watch Adventist TV and was certain no one would come and stand in front of a screen in a church and give his or her heart to the Lord. He admits being so skeptical that during the broadcast of NET '96, he would put in a tape for the broadcast and then jump on his motorcycle and ride about 3.5 miles (about 6 kilometers) to the Adventist church in Novo Friburgo just to see if there really was an audience.

To Jorge's amazement, each night, people came and followed the messages carefully. By the end of the series, he was "converted" to satellite evangelism—convinced that it really worked! The same was true of thousands of others in South America, as they saw the evidence of the power of Adventist television ministry.

Pastor Braun, Pastor Williams Costa, Jr., Sonete, Marcelo, Jorge, Jonatan, Tennison, and many others spent countless hours working to build the TV ministry in South America. In the early days, the uplink and broadcast were not automated and required long hours of manually inserting tapes for broadcast. Jorge laughs and recalls how he would work eighteen to twenty hours with no break, inserting tapes every half hour or hour as needed. "That was before I was married and had my daughter!" he says.

Why did these young pioneers do this? God had opened doors, and they were determined to be faithful and expand His work as much as possible.

The results

Indeed, God's leading is evident in the South American TV ministry. Through the strong, visionary support of Pastor Nagel, president of the South American Division, and of Pastor Bullón and many other key church leaders, the tiny media center dedicated to radio, TV, and Bible school ministry has grown today into a dynamic, vibrant, and flourishing ministry. Visitors are thrilled with the enthusiasm and dedication of the talented team who run it.

In many respects, South American Adventist Television Network operations lead the world. Daily TV production, satellite evangelism, expanding distribution, and hundreds of viewer responses every day testify to the powerful blessing of God. Some of the highlights of this amazing story follow:

Adventist Satellite (ADSAT) headquarters in Nova Friburgo

- In less than five years, the South American Adventist Church network grew to more than six thousand church and institution downlink locations in Brazil alone, servicing the Portuguese-speaking members. The Spanish downlink network adds several thousand more sites.
- From the small start of NET '96, by 2005, nearly two dozen major satellite evangelism series have added nearly five hundred thousand new brothers and sisters to the church family.
- Every year, Adventist Church leadership uses the TV network extensively for training and communication with the churches of South America.
- The full-time Portuguese TV channel continues to grow rapidly.
- A full-time Spanish language Esperanza Channel is expanding.
- By 2005, nearly two hundred cable networks and low-power TV stations were broadcasting the Hope channels.
- The media center in Novo Friburgo produces two hours of new TV programming daily.
- Through the kindness of Dr. Afonso, media centers have opened in Argentina, Bolivia, Chile, and Peru.
- Brazil has seen the opening of twelve additional smaller TV media centers, which produce programming for the broadcasts.

- The church's major South American colleges and universities have developed extensive video-production curriculums for their communication majors.
- Through the kindness of Dr. Afonso, the church has obtained "open" TV licenses in the largest cities of Chile.
- Extensive cable network redistribution of the Spanish Hope Channel is taking place in many Spanish-speaking countries of South America.

The success God has given in South America is a powerful encouragement. Starting a full-time TV ministry is not easy. This story portrays what persistence, faith, and hard work, coupled with the Lord's blessing can accomplish. God does amazing things.

Today, Pastors Milton Souza, Williams Costa, Jr., and Flavio Ferraz manage the media center, which employs more than one hundred people. TV production and uplink is soon to move to a new, larger facility. And both the Portuguese and Spanish Hope Channels have become powerful tools for evangelism and discipling. They elicit hundreds of responses from viewers each day.

Now, satellite evangelistic events are adding tens of thousands of people to the church each year. Truly, God intended Adventists to draw the honest seekers for truth to His church through the powerful medium of television.

Pacific Rim

God has plans that often reach beyond the scope of our imagination and perspectives. Following the success of NET '95 and '96 in North and South America and Europe, Adventist Church leaders pondered the possibility of extending satellite evangelism to other regions of the world. Since people in Australia and some of the South Pacific islands speak English primarily, it seemed reasonable they could also participate in this exciting new methodology. But what about the diverse cultures and languages of China, Korea, Japan, and Taiwan? Could they benefit from satellite NET evangelism?

Some people emphatically stated that though satellite evangelism had been successful in the Americas and Europe, it couldn't possibly work in the South Pacific. They questioned the cultural appropriateness of a first-world program coming to third-world countries such as Papua New Guinea. And they noted that Australia is very secular and not overly sympathetic to American ideology, particularly when it comes to religious matters. There were also technical questions to solve: Which satellite would we use? What size of antenna would be necessary? And what about the significant time differences between the many time zones of the Pacific Rim? However, in faith, church leaders laid plans to participate in NET '98.

As word went out that NET '98 would be broadcast to this area of the world, church members got behind the project. Despite the unknowns, they too wanted to be part of the global Adventist family and share in this unique evangelism. Churches in scores of sites in Australia and New Zealand purchased the 9-foot (2.8-meter) satellite dishes and installed them. What happened in the ensuing months was a miracle, as people filled churches and large stadiums to hear the message of the gospel via satellite from half a world away.

Australia, October 1998

We had a clear indication that God was behind the project when He providentially directed the political affairs of Australia days before the start of NET '98. In an article for the South Pacific Division *Record,* Pastor Ray Coombe, satellite coordinator for that division, told the story:

> Without the distraction of a conflicting federal election (praise God), NET '98 will commence on Saturday afternoon or night on October 10. It is rather exciting to see God's hand in this matter. For several months, political pundits have been predicting the possibility of an Australian Federal Election on October 10 or 17. What they never knew—and Mr. Howard himself did not realize—is that for many months, October 10 was already booked as the start of "The NeXt Millennium Seminar."
>
> In spite of the fact that October 3 is in the school holidays, and a long weekend in several states, Prime Minister Howard, to the surprise of many, chose that date (not October 10) for the national election! We believe that God would not have it otherwise, and the beginning of NET '98 will not have to compete with the distraction and frenzy of a polling day. NET '98 comes at a time when people are desperately searching for security and hope.

Papua New Guinea, March 1998

Satellite downlink equipment was not easily available in Papua New Guinea in 1998. Pastor Les and Mary Lane Anderson from California were shipping their personal possessions to Papua New Guinea in a container. Les was a skilled pilot, and the Andersons were joining the Adventist Aviation Ministry in that country. Kindly, they consented to take several sets of satellite downlink equipment with them for the NET '98 event and assisted in their installation.

The results? Papua New Guinea satellite coordinator Pastor Diave reported via email:

> In Lae, the crowd is swelling past the 20,000 mark as we move from the stadium to the Eriku Oval. First night at Eriku was 20,000 and last night the crowd has swelled to over 30,000. Some were even sitting at the bus stop on the other side of the oval, and mind you, this oval contains about 4 softball diamonds. Port Moresby is also

experiencing that type of crowd, reaching over 40,000. Mt. Hagen is going steady with an audience between 10–15,000. The "small" locations have 6–7,000.

The response of audiences in Papua New Guinea to NET '98 completely shocked everyone. In spite of heavy rains and a half-dozen meeting locations, their enthusiasm was unmatched. Tapes of each night's broadcast were couriered to key locations across the country from the Adventist Media Center in Sydney, Australia, and then taken to sports stadiums, where audiences packed in to hear and watch the messages from the sky.

Adventist mission pilot Les Anderson, who, with his wife, Mary Lane, brought downlink equipment to Papua New Guinea

Quite some time later, the following story came to us from Pastor Willie Grobler of the Adelaide City Church via Malcolm and Gladys Leonie, satellite coordinators in South Africa: About twenty men from Papua New Guinea walked into the Adelaide City Church on Sabbath, October 2, 1999, and sat in the front few pews. Just before the Sabbath School superintendent started her program, one of the men offered for the group to sing a special number. The superintendent said Yes, they sang, and the performance was great. So they were asked to sing during the worship service as well.

Then church members asked where they were from and whether they were a touring choir. They answered, "We are the Papua New Guinea rugby team, and we're in Adelaide to play in the International Masters Games."

For these games, men and women who used to be professional and semi-professional players in their sports come to South Australia to compete. At least twenty countries were there for this particular competition. The team told the church, "We play New Zealand tonight, and we're gonna beat them."

Then church members asked, "Why did you come to the Adventist church this Saturday morning?"

"Well," the team answered, "the entire rugby team is now Seventh-day Adventist. We were scheduled to play against New Zealand this afternoon, but we told them we couldn't on our Sabbath, so they've rescheduled the game for tonight."

The team was from the first church founded in Papua New Guinea by missionaries and Kata Rangoso (of "Fuzzy Wuzzy Angels" fame in WWII). The membership of that church is now about fifteen hundred. They said that the 1998 satellite downlink of Dwight Nelson drew such large crowds that the church had to hire a few stadiums throughout the country. Nearly sixty thousand people came to the satellite services in their area. So many people became members that the church was conducting baptisms of hundreds of people throughout the series.

Japan, October 1998

Pastor Machida from Okinawa reported:

> Praise the Lord for the success of the first worldwide NET '98 broadcast at Pioneer Memorial Church! Thank you very much for your patience and hard work. In Okinawa, a total of twenty churches and companies [are] participat[ing]. . . . Nearly half of the audiences are visitors. . . . It is really great to be part of the Adventist global family.

During NET '98, a businessperson from Argentina was in Japan on business. Somehow, he learned of the satellite series and began attending in one of the Okinawa locations. The members were excited to have him as a guest. He didn't speak either Japanese or English, so they set up a TV in another room and tuned it to the Spanish translation. During the series, this man gave his heart to Christ. From Argentina, through the ministry of Pastor Dwight Nelson in North America, via satellite in Japan!

Papua New Guinea, July 2001

After NET '98, the satellite ministry in Papua New Guinea grew rapidly. People were mesmerized by the fact that with today's technology and the help of the Holy Spirit, Pastor Dwight Nelson spoke in Pidgin. Pastor Matupit Darius had flown to Andrews University and provided simultaneous translation for NET '98. Poor Pastor Darius never had seen snow before, and he found the winter weather of Michigan extremely cold. He suffered, but the viewers in Papua New Guinea rejoiced.

In various email reports, Papua New Guinea satellite coordinator Pastor Diave faithfully kept ATN updated on satellite-evangelism developments. (The following report has been lightly edited to make a narrative.)

When the word got around that the last ACTS 2000 series, Revelation of Hope, would be hosted in Port Moresby, Papua New Guinea, everybody was excited. By the time the series started, there were more than fifty downlink sites in the country. In addition, the entire series was rebroadcast on national TV and radio.

A young woman who was enrolled in a teachers college in Madang began attending the satellite program there. She was so interested that she enrolled in the baptismal class. When it was time for her college graduation, her parents came to witness the event. She decided to tell them about her decision to be baptized only after the graduation, so as not to spoil the party. When she did tell them, she struggled to get the words out, knowing her parents were dedicated members of another denomination. Much to her surprise, they responded with both smiles and tears.

Pastor Mark Finley preaches following ACTS— Papua New Guinea

It turns out that the tears were tears of joy. The parents confided to their daughter that they had attended the satellite meetings where they lived and they had also decided to be baptized as Seventh-day Adventists.

In Lae, an eight-year-old lad named Dixon noticed that there was a big work bee in one of the stadiums. A stage was being built and giant screens were being raised. After inquiring about what was happening, Dixon went home to tell his mother the exciting news that the Adventist Church would be running a program via satellite, and he urged his mother to take him to the meeting. Though his mother filled her evenings playing cards and selling betel nut, she half-heartedly agreed.

However, when it was time for the satellite program to start, she was so busy with her activities that she didn't want to go. When Dixon realized his mum wouldn't go with him, he made his way to the program alone. He did this every night. Each night he would come home and report the happenings to his mother. She would promise him that she would go with him the next night. Unfortunately, she never did, and then the program ended.

On the Thursday after the program concluded, Dixon was climbing a guava tree, picking the ripe fruits, when suddenly an earthquake shook the whole place. His mother, still busy playing cards, looked up and saw her son up in the tree. She started wailing for him to come down lest the earthquake shake him down. But Dixon was enjoying riding out the earthquake while sitting in the tree. He told his mother, "You are worried about me in a tree during an earthquake, but you never were concerned about me when I asked you last week to come to the meetings with me. Had you attended those meetings, you wouldn't be as worried as you are now."

That reply shook his mother to the bones. She began to think, My son has some faith that I don't have. What shall I do? Then she asked Dixon where the nearest Adventist church was, and, much to his surprise, she promised him that they would go to church together.

Come Sabbath morning, Dixon took a shower. Then he encouraged his mum to do the same, and, reluctantly, she obeyed her son. They put on the best clothes that they could find and made their way to church.

Dixon went in to the primary class, where he had become a regular attendee. His mum was having trouble with the thought that no one would welcome her to the church. She breathed a prayer for help. Then the warmth of the deacons and deaconesses who were greeters at the door of the church encompassed her, and she felt that she wanted to sit in the front, not at the back.

A year later, Dixon was able to stand by his mother's side as through baptism she publicly showed the world that she was a follower of Jesus Christ. Dixon's mum is now a deaconess, and since the first day she entered the church, her place is in the front seats.

Korea, November 2003

In 2003–2004, the Seventh-day Adventist Church in Korea celebrated the centennial of its start in that country. Through the years, many significant developments have contributed to the dynamic growth of the church there to nearly seven hundred Adventist churches and more than 167,000 members. The Korean church operates Sahmyook University, a major printing/publishing house, a health-food factory, a media center, and many other facilities.

In commemoration of the blessings of God during the past one hundred years, the Korean church initiated a major satellite NET evangelism event and invited Pastor Doug Batchelor, director/speaker of Amazing Facts, to conduct the meetings from Sahmyook University. This event involved churches across the Pacific Rim region, but particularly within Korea. Some 558 churches in Korea participated at four hundred downlink sites.

Sometimes, adjusting to the new technology proved amusing. One saintly eighty-two-year-old deaconess watched the opening-night meeting at her church's downlink site. After the meeting, church members found her busily looking for rice to prepare a meal. Confused about what she was doing, they asked her why she wanted to prepare the rice. She responded that they must prepare food for

Koreans paid close attention during Pastor Doug Batchelor's series

the visiting pastor. They then explained that Pastor Batchelor was in Seoul and had come to their church via satellite broadcast. What she had seen was his picture on a screen.

Particularly significant in this event was the extensive use of the Internet for streaming video distribution. Sufficient bandwidth was available in many locations to support good quality, large-screen projection of the program via Internet. This was a first for the world Adventist Television Network and reveals a significant way the Adventist Church can use Internet technology in the future.

More than twenty-two thousand people attended the series nightly in Korea, experiencing the power of God through the preaching of Pastor Batchelor. Amazing Facts reports that more than four thousand people were baptized and became members of the Adventist Church through the series. Amazing Facts recounts the following experiences:

A woman who had been a Buddhist all her life responded to Pastor Doug's appeal after the fifth night and requested baptism. When the Adventist pastor came to visit her, she had gotten rid of all her idols. She said, "I don't need them anymore because I worship the true God now." She and her husband were both baptized.

A mother of two small children started to attend the meetings and enjoyed each program. The morning of the third day of the meetings, both children woke up ill; the three-year-old had a fever, and the six-year-old had broken out with red spots on his body. The mother prayed all afternoon that God would heal her children so she could attend the meetings. In faith, she went that night, taking her children. By the time she arrived at the meeting site, both children had been miraculously healed.

Baptism in Korea during an ACTS 2000 series

One of the world's largest Christian churches is located in Korea. The head deaconess of that church said that after she heard the message on the Bible Sabbath, she couldn't sleep. All night she wrestled with the conviction that what she had learned was truth. By morning, her struggle was over; she had decided to follow God's teaching regarding the Sabbath. She and a friend, also a deaconess from another church, were baptized as Seventh-day Adventists.

In 2003, with the development of the Hope Channel full-time broadcasts, God providentially provided satellite space sufficient for three separate channels for the Pacific Rim. Currently, the English Hope Channel International is the only Hope Channel broadcast full time to this vast region. Presently, church leadership around the Pacific Rim is working closely with Hope Channel to open Hope Channel—Asia soon. The Chinese culture is pervasive in many countries of the Pacific Rim. We must meet the cultural and linguistic distinctiveness of this large region of the world with appropriately contextualized programming in the languages of these countries. "This gospel of the kingdom shall be preached in all the world for a witness unto all nations; and then shall the end come" (Matthew 24:14, KJV).

Australia, New Zealand, Papua New Guinea, Samoa, Fiji, Oceania, Southeast Asia, Indonesia, Philippines, Hong Kong, Guam, Korea, Japan, Eastern Siberia—across the vast, diverse Pacific Rim, several thousand churches have installed satellite dishes. The ATN network is regularly used for satellite NET events and Hope Channel International, and thousands have been baptized as a result.

Africa

Following the success of NET '95 in North America and NET '96 in North and South America and Europe, Pastor Robert Folkenberg, then president of the General Conference, dreamed of satellite NET evangelism coming to Africa. After Pastor Folkenberg shared his dream with Pastor Wakaba, president of the South Africa Union of the Seventh-day Adventist Church, the union committed to hosting the first African satellite NET series. Lay evangelist Fitz Henry of Jamaica was invited to be the speaker. The host site was the large Vista University auditorium in Soweto, a township close to Johannesburg. The satellite NET evangelism event was named Pentecost '98.

In establishing a church satellite TV network in Africa for this event, the Adventist Television Network faced formidable challenges: Communication and transportation over vast distances, lack of widespread technical knowledge of electronics, lack of availability of equipment, economic disparity, and cultural differences. In addition, many countries in Africa have very limited television infrastructure.

The church of Africa was starting at ground zero in satellite NET evangelism. We would have to establish every aspect of the network there. And methods used in other areas of the world wouldn't necessarily work in Africa. Church leaders had to encourage and organize local church awareness, preparation, and participation. They needed to find, deliver, and install economically priced equipment. They had to develop and implement training for installation and operation of the equipment in hundreds of locations spread across thousands of miles. They also had to develop and implement a practical technical support organization.

In addition, they needed to prepare the site of the local host meetings. Someone had to build a TV-ready backdrop. A unified advertising campaign such as the church had never before done in Africa needed to be developed, printed, and distributed. And they needed to find translators, secure visas for them, and arrange their travel to Johannesburg. The list seemed to go on and on.

Adding to these challenges was the time frame. It was short. The South African Union did extensive preparation among its churches in advance, but the schedule initially called for the final prepa-

The author and family with Pastor Phil Follett during Pentecost '98

ration—the technical, training, and organizational aspects across Africa— to be done in a little less than three months. Resolving these challenges for Pentecost '98 required Heaven's intervention. The following is a very brief summary of some of the greatest challenges and how God intervened to establish the ATN network in Africa.

South Africa, January 1998

"Impossible! Mr. Thorp, what you want to do in Africa is not possible. It simply can't be done this soon. There is no way the Adventist Church can develop a satellite network across Africa in just a few weeks. It won't happen." Mr. Bretherick shook his head slowly.

We had been referred to Peter Bretherick, president of the Telemedia Company in Johannesburg. Mr. Bretherick is a leading specialist in satellite broadcast in Africa. His company has extensive experience in uplinking events from many African countries. He is very knowledgeable about the industry, well connected, a successful businessperson, and knows Africa well.

Days before, we had heard the story of a major oil company installing a satellite business network in Africa. After three years and many difficulties, they had succeeded in establishing only forty downlink sites. Certainly, a large corporation had far more financial resources and capability than the Adventist Church had for this new project. We needed to install hundreds of locations, and in less than three months. How would God help His church? How would the Lord provide to make this dream possible?

In a visit to Africa in mid-1997, Brad had shared the NET concept. Church leaders in South Africa had caught the vision of the whole project and had appointed a technical team led by Nolleen Johnson to determine what was needed and to find the equipment. Tirelessly, Nolleen and her volunteer technical team visited scores of churches, enthusiastically promoting satellite evangelism, answering questions, and providing technical guidance.

Elephants and satellite signals

Convincing churches across Africa to get involved was not easy. Each congregation had to fund the purchase of its own equipment; there were no subsidies from regional Adventist headquarters. Unemployment plagues the majority of African countries, and where people can work, the average income is approximately fifty dollars per month.

As Brad traveled to numerous countries, it soon became evident that many people found the idea of satellite evangelism foreign and difficult to understand. There was little with which to compare it. Only a few relatively wealthy people in cities had satellite dishes. At an Adventist Church convocation in central Botswana, Brad shared the stories of NET '95 and '96. People listened attentively. But when he began to explain how the satellite equipment worked and how they would be able to participate in Pentecost '98 from Soweto, people shook their heads and sat unbelieving, their faces blank. How could signals from the sky bring them sermons that they could see and hear?

Pastor Lekolwane, who was translating for Brad, came to the rescue. He said, "Brad, give me a few moments to explain this technology in a way the people can understand." Then, with a mischievous grin that stretched from ear to ear, he told the audience, "Imagine a big elephant flapping its ears toward the sky. His ears are the satellite dish. The elephant's trunk is the LNB that understands the message from the sky. The satellite equipment will bring you music and preaching all the way from South Africa here to your church."

The people laughed and cheered. They wanted to be part of this new venture of their Adventist Church. But how could it happen? Where could we find the equipment? How would we ever communicate the necessary information to all the countries? How could the churches raise the necessary funds? There were many unanswered questions, and the clock continued to tick.

At that time, consumer-grade digital receivers were unreliable and generally unavailable anyway. The receivers had to come from North America and would be drop-shipped to each country when an order was confirmed. Video projectors were very expensive and not readily available. Eventually, we determined that we could obtain the best kind of projector from Ernst Seegler in Europe. It was only a 50 Ansi lumen video projector. (By today's standard, this seems weak, yet many of these projectors are still functioning and give a good picture at night.) And Warren Judd and Peter Bretherick determined that the churches in most of Africa needed a minimum 7.5-foot (2.3-meter) antenna. Satellite dishes were not readily available at that time in many African countries. Where would we find this equipment?

In late 1997, the Lord opened an interesting door that provided many South African churches with good, used satellite dishes. Pastor François Louw, who was pastoring in the Cape Town area, had a good relationship with the regional bank manager for ABSA bank. One day they were discussing technology, and the manager casually mentioned that ABSA would soon be phasing out their C-band satellite communication network. Pastor Louw immediately asked what they would do with all the used satellite equipment. The manager said the bank would sell the equipment to whoever made a reasonable offer.

Pastor Louw asked for an inventory of what equipment was available and where it was located. He discovered that the bank had originally imported the antennas from the United States, and, including installation, it had cost ABSA more than five thousand dollars per location.

Pastor Louw offered ABSA a thousand rands (two hundred dollars) for each system. ABSA accepted this offer, and all across South Africa, our members simply went to the nearest ABSA bank that had this equipment. They carefully dismantled the antennas and took everything: the

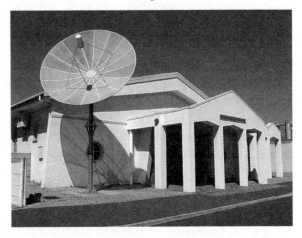

The Tygerberg, South Africa, church with an ABSA satellite dish

stands, pole, mounting brackets, cabling, and LNBs. In this way, nearly 150 Adventist churches in South Africa obtained satellite systems for a fraction of the original cost.

Pastor Louw remembers, "Definitely, the ABSA dishes were a miracle! It gave the Adventist churches immediate access to the best satellite equipment in the country at that time. Providentially, it was exactly the equipment we needed for satellite evangelism."

God had provided a solution for South Africa; now, what would He do for the rest of the continent?

Serious problems finding equipment

For days, we wrestled with the serious problem of obtaining satellite dishes for the part of the continent outside South Africa. We thought about chartering an airplane and sending it through the various countries. It wouldn't work.

During the day, Brad pursued every possible lead throughout Africa and India, spending hours on the phone. Many nights, during business hours in the United States, we slept little as he spent more hours on the phone, trying to find a solution there. He explored every option thoroughly, only to repeatedly come up to a dead end. We couldn't find a satisfactory source for the antennas. Maybe we really couldn't do satellite evangelism in Africa.

Earnestly, we prayed daily for an answer, and we solicited the persistent prayers of others across North America, Europe, and Africa. With no solution forthcoming and nearly every possible avenue exhausted, we felt as if we were beating our heads against a huge brick wall. Surely, God wouldn't lead His church this far just to let it fail. But it seemed we were blocked on every side and the project was doomed.

Finally, a breakthrough came. We found a local supplier for some of the countries in eastern Africa. At the same time, we discovered that the SAMI company, located in Arkansas in the United States, made a satellite dish of the right size. This dish came in a standard-size box, ready for UPS shipment, and UPS would drop ship into Africa at a reasonable price, satisfactorily covering the needs for western and central Africa. Praise God, He had provided a solution, but time was not on our side.

Brad realized that another key factor to the success of the whole project lay in the local church members installing their own equipment. This would facilitate local ownership and training to operate the equipment. We needed to develop a manual with pictures and simple instructions.

Errol Van Eck, an elder in the Sandton church, volunteered. His manual proved to be extremely useful in the months and years that followed. (See <http://adventist.tv/techinfo/Equipmt/installing/indexmanual.htm>.)

Pentecost '98 Vista University miracle

As the days ticked by, amazingly, more and more orders for equipment came in from around the continent. However, it quickly became evident that the equipment wouldn't be delivered and installed in time. Only a few sites in South Africa and possibly eastern Africa would be prepared. We needed more time. Nearly five hundred churches had raised the necessary funds and wanted to participate. There was no way the series could begin as scheduled on February 25 and be successful. Pastor Luka Daniel, president of the Adventist Church in West Africa, urged the team to consider permitting a couple more months of preparation. But could the date be delayed?

A "Home of Hope" in Lesotho

Pastor Wakaba and the other Adventist Church leaders and evangelist Fitz Henry were sympathetic and agreed graciously to delay the start of Pentecost '98 if necessary. We would need a providential act of God's guidance to show the direction to take. Many prayers ascended to heaven for God to make the way clear.

Miraculously, the answer came through the administrators of Vista University in Soweto. The university had made unusual concessions to allow for the original February date. They had fitted their academic programs around the dates of Pentecost '98. In an email, Brad reported what transpired. He wrote: "Today, January 13, a delegation of the church leadership visited Vista University, . . . and [Vista officials] have agreed to accommodate a later starting date. . . . This is a very gracious move on the part of the university, which we deeply appreciate, and in our view is a providential act of God."

The series was postponed to a start date of April 25, allowing two extra months of preparation. What happened across Africa in the ensuing months was unprecedented. In spite of challenges in clearing the valuable equipment through customs and the complexity of using multiple shipping services, the churches got their prized equipment. In many locations around the continent, anxious elders and deacons who had little technical background installed the equipment. When the installers carefully followed the manual Errol Van Eck had prepared, they consistently had little difficulty in getting properly "tuned in." The reports we received implied that in more than one instance, the angels assisted in helping the operators find the satellite and the program from the sky.

Challenges and more challenges

At this time, communication was very, very difficult. There was virtually no email network across Africa. Cellular telephone service was limited, and landline phone connections weren't very dependable.

Ray Cloete, the Adventist advertising specialist responsible for designing all the advertising for Pentecost '98, was robbed at gunpoint in his home just weeks before the campaign. Thankfully, the bullets never found their target, as if angels shielded him. However, the entire family was traumatized, and for several days we wondered if the advertising would be done in time. But it was completed, though with hardly a day to go.

In March, we compiled organizational manuals, advertising, and instructional videos, which we shipped to twenty-two countries. It took days of work plus the help of our two younger sons and volunteers from the Sandton church to collate the tens of thousands of pieces of paper into the manuals and pack all the boxes for the DHL courier. I remember this shipment resulting in the most expensive courier bill ATN ever paid.

Miracle after miracle occurred. One by one, the "insurmountable" challenges were met and overcome. The support of the local Adventist church leadership and community was amazing. Brad's mother passed away exactly one week before the meetings started. A delayed funeral was arranged. In a special way, we will always remember the compassionate ministry of Louis and Marilyn Van Aswegen and Pastor Daniel Latchman during this difficult time.

Impossible? Possible with God!

April 25, 1998, will remain a very special day to us. The first African satellite meeting, broadcast in sixteen languages, was successfully launched.

By God's grace, the impossible was accomplished! Opening night, fourteen weeks after we began to obtain and install equipment, hundreds of satellite downlink sites successfully tuned into Pentecost '98 from Soweto. Hundreds of pastors and thousands of church members had successfully prepared their churches and communities, and they welcomed tens of thousands of visitors to the meetings. This was a miracle.

In an email to Pastors Folkenberg, Follett, and Don Robinson, Brad reported:

> The overall program went smoothly. . . . We have made an excellent start. We have the network established in Africa. This is such a big relief!!!!! PTL. Not all locations are OK—but they will be in the next few days. Many countries have reported a response. Many large attendances are reported. God has been most good to us and I am thankful for His blessing. Thank you for remembering us in your prayers.

Pastor Ray Zeeman, Pentecost '98 coordinator for South Africa, wrote in an email to Brad:

> The good hand of the Lord was upon everything and it was an outstanding success. While in Cape Town I attended two sites on the opening night viz. Riverside and Athlone. It was absolute magic. The churches were just about completely full and everyone was glued to the big screen. The picture and sound was perfect. The effectiveness of the satellite-evangelism program exceeded my wildest imagination. I am completely sold over to the idea. The enthusiastic participation of the congregations without any prodding is unbelievable.

Another surprise awaited the host site team the opening weekend. Coming by van all the way from Tanzania were Pastors Mbwana, Bina, and Mutani, Adventist Church leaders from Tanzania. They drove more than 1,800 miles (3,000 kilometers) over difficult roads to see for themselves exactly what was happening.

Without fully understanding the project, in faith, the Adventist Church in Tanzania established more than forty sites for Pentecost '98. Some of the locations were so rural that when the satellite series began, people walked hours over the mountain trails to reach the location of a downlink. In some of the remote Tanzanian locations, to give information to the coordinators, a deacon had to ride his bike more than a day to get to the site.

Audiences in some locations far exceeded expectations. Reports faxed from Rwanda indicated that in the site run by the Remero church in Kigali, the audience exceeded twenty thousand! Brother Fitz Henry endeared himself to this audience by welcoming them each evening with "Good evening, Kigaaalii!" Many churches set up their equipment outside the church structure to accommodate hundreds more than could ever fit inside.

Just as incredible were the reports from small downlink sites. Pastor Nation Xhamela reported that the Thembalethu church in Cape Town had a membership of 250 and baptized more than 279 people during Pentecost '98. Pastor Chris Botha, president of the Adventist Church in the Transvaal region of South Africa, told of seven elderly women in northern Transvaal who with great sacrifice bought the equipment for their little home church and were thrilled that twenty to twenty-five guests attended every night. And in a May 13 email report, Pastor Weiers Coetser noted:

> The Phoenix SDA church does not have a church building; neither did we have the money to acquire the satellite equipment. But one of our (unemployed) church members sacrificed a great deal and bought the dish and the receiver. Now we worship in his house with televisions in the garage, the living room, and the dining room. Every evening about fifty people attend (twenty to twenty-five visitors). People walk up to five kilometers [about three miles] to attend the evening programs.

In a brief report that Pastor Ray Zeeman wrote at the conclusion of Pentecost '98, he said:

> Pentecost '98, the newest and the biggest evangelistic campaign ever conducted by our union [the South Africa Union], was an unqualified success. With the blessings of the Lord very evident, and employing satellite technology, over 20,000 people attended the evangelistic meetings at 150 downlink sites across our union. This resulted in the biggest baptism ever, with 4,410 souls baptized as of the end of June. We praise God for this abundant harvest. Pentecost '98 welded the churches and their leaders into one huge

international team, intent on winning the greatest number of persons to the Savior. Particularly heartening and outstanding was the wonderful support and involvement by lay leaders in the local churches. Across the rest of the continent of Africa, an additional 13,000 souls were baptized, with 6,000 more in baptismal classes. The final combined number of souls baptized from Pentecost '98 is expected to be approximately 23,000 persons. Pentecost '98 has recovered soul winning as the most important mission of the church. What a privilege it was for South Africa and the SAU [South African Union] to host this wonderfully successful evangelistic campaign.

Three hundred fifty-seven sites tune in
On the final weekend of Pentecost '98, Brad reported:

This series has been a tremendous challenge—organizationally and technically. But our God is greater! And praise to His Holy name and the work of the Holy Spirit, He has won a great victory. . . . A total of 472 sets of equipment were ordered. For Africa and its economies this represents tremendous sacrifice and commitment. Due to a variety of transportation, customs, and technical problems as best we can document, 357 sites actually were installed and received the program live. The last country and site to come "on line" was Burundi and the capital of Bujumbura. This final Sabbath morning they received their first telecast for the Sabbath morning service and were able to get the last two broadcasts live.

During the series, Peter Bretherick sat in his office, watching the live program that his company, Telemedia, was uplinking from Soweto for us. He told Brad, "What you people have done is simply amazing. To have more than three hundred sites across Africa installed in less than four months is really astonishing."

Remarkable? No—miraculous!

Nothing is impossible with God, and the development of satellite evangelism in Africa is indeed extraordinary evidence of Heaven's interest in the venture. Downlinks were established in locations where there was no TV, no telephones, and no electricity. With the aid of a small generator, Adventist church members would switch on their satellite equipment, offering the community an unrivaled evangelistic program.

Eager listeners at the series hosted at Vista University

No one dreamed that in less than six years, more than two thousand Adventist Church locations across Africa would be equipped, Adventists would be manufacturing satellite dishes, and thousands of private locations would be tuned to Hope Channel. The satellite audience of approximately 250,000 for Pentecost '98 would grow to become audiences of more than a million viewers in later satellite events. The estimated twenty-five thousand baptisms from Pentecost '98 would increase to tens of thousands from the eight major satellite NET events conducted to date in Africa using this technology. No wonder it was so difficult!

Envisioning the enlargement of ATN from occasional Adventist Church broadcasts to full-time, in-home television by Hope Channel International, Pastor Pardon Mwansa, president of the Southern African–Indian Ocean Division of the Seventh-day Adventist Church, challenged, "Give us Adventist Television in the homes of our people. You cannot imagine what will happen when our members begin going from door to door, asking their friends and neighbors if they are watching Hope Channel."

In addition to continued satellite-evangelism events, today, ATN is establishing a low-power TV network across Africa, on which millions will daily view Hope Channel International.

Epilogue:

The Hope Channels— Windows for the World

The start, development, and rapid spread around the world of the Adventist Television Network (ATN) is clearly the result of God's miraculous leading. As evidenced in this book, time after time we have seen God miraculously intervene, performing miracles for the sharing of the gospel through this new, innovative method called satellite NET evangelism.

Through satellite NET evangelism, the church has proclaimed the gospel message in nearly sixty languages and to about 150 countries. As Adventist Church members around the world have experienced this mode of evangelism, they've begun a "grassroots, ground-swell" request for the world church to start full-time, in-home Adventist television. At the same time, God providentially arranged for satellite contracts and technical developments to permit the corporate church to begin full-time global broadcast. Church leadership intends for Adventist TV to represent the multinational, multicultural diversity of the global Adventist Church. ATN is to provide opportunity for creative and effective expression of the varied spiritual gifts in the world church.

Now, as in the diverse satellite NET evangelism events, the mandate of ATN is to present through the Hope Channels programming that is contextualized to the local culture as much as possible. Hope Channel programs are designed to attract the largest audience possible of spiritually sensitive viewers and to nurture and disciple the worldwide Adventist Church family. Hope Channel is the official television voice of the world Adventist Church. It aims to benefit both members and nonmembers.

Providentially, in a very short time, the Adventist Church has begun operating six different Hope channels:

- Esperança (Portuguese; South America; begun early in 2002)
- Esperanza (Spanish; South America; begun late in 2003)
- Hope Channel (English; North America and Inter-America; begun late in 2003)
- Esperanza TV (Spanish and French; North America and Inter-America; July 2004)
- Hope Channel International (English; November 2004)
- Hope Channel Europe (Multilanguage; May 2005)

Plans are in development for additional Hope channels to target major people groups.
- Hope Channel Asia (1)
- Hope Channel Asia (2)
- Hope Channel Africa (Portuguese and French)

Fundamentally, the Hope channels are intended to function as an attractive window through which the world can see the tremendous blessings and wonderful message God has entrusted to the global Adventist Church, as evidenced in our quality of life, unity, and growth. In a world torn by international war, family strife, and private pain, God intends the totality of witness provided by His multicultural, international, spiritual family to testify to the appealing power of His way of life, to give a genuine message of hope. "You are my witnesses" (Isaiah 43:10, NIV) takes on new meaning when we consider the potential in a global church family that demonstrates God's way of life in a multiplicity of contexts.

Hope Channel programming is intended to be unique. The goal is not simply to promote individuals, a ministry, a project, or fund-raising or to satisfy the desires of a narrow demographic group. It is to accomplish the mission of proclaiming and providing a realistic, practical demonstration of biblical truth to spiritually receptive individuals worldwide.

Hope Channel programming is inclusive. It is intended to appeal to anyone regardless of race, color, or creed who is open to the principles and teachings God has revealed.

Hope Channel opens a new paradigm of communication for the world Adventist Church. Previously, Adventist Church TV productions have consisted of "specials" broadcast occasionally on time purchased from TV stations. With the Hope channels, Adventist Church communication can now include full-time TV programming in any community.

Hope Channel is for you, your family, and friends! Messages promoting values opposed to the genuine principles of truth and successful living bombard us constantly. Hope Channel is intended to provide you with a fresh, realistic, practical, and joyful television alternative that brings peace and hope to your life.

Every day, Hope Channel receives hundreds of prayer requests and comments. Many viewers say that God is changing and transforming their life. We are thrilled that the programs of Hope Channel are such a blessing, and we encourage you to share in these benefits. "May the God of hope fill you with all joy and peace as you trust in him, so that you may overflow with hope by the power of the Holy Spirit" (Romans 15:13, NIV).

How You Can Help

People often ask us how they can share in the work of the Hope channels. There are several ways:
- Pray for the Hope channels.
- Install an antenna dish for your home and watch Hope Channel yourself.
- Visit our Web site: <www.HopeTV.org>.
- Subscribe to our monthly newsletter and email letter.
- Tell others about and invite them to watch Hope Channel.
- Send a letter to your local television providers (TV station, cable company, direct-to-home, small-dish company) and ask them to add Hope Channel to their line-up.
- Provide financial support to Hope Channel.
- Volunteer to assist Hope Channel. Currently, volunteers help in a wide range of technical and production roles.

Contact Information

Postal address:	The Hope Channel
	P.O. Box 4000
	Silver Spring, MD 20914
Telephone:	301-680-6689
Web site:	www.HopeTV.org
Email:	info@HopeTV.org (for general information)
	comments@HopeTV.org (for comments on our programs)
	prayer@HopeTV.org (for prayer requests)

Have you experienced a miracle?

Have you or your church experienced a miracle in connection with satellite NET evangelism or the Hope Channels? If so, we would appreciate hearing from you and may, where appropriate, share your experience with others. Contact us with details at

Email: Miracles@HopeTV.org
Postal mail: Miracles
                             Hope Channel
                             P.O. Box 4000
                             Silver Spring, MD 20914

Please enclose your name, address, telephone number, and contact information so we can contact you.

Appendix:

ATN Satellite Evangelism Events, 1995–2005

Appendix

#	Name	Date	Host Location	Speaker	Coverage
			1995		
1	NET '95	Mar 1995	Chattanooga, TN, USA	M Finley	North America
			1996		
2	NET '96	Oct 1996	Orlando, FL, USA	M Finley	North America
			1997		
3	Hope Beyond 2000	Nov 1997	Seattle, WA, USA	K Cox	North America
			1998		
4		Apr 1998	Panama	A Bullón	ADSAT*
5	Pentecost '98	Apr 1998	Soweto, South Africa	F Henry	Africa
6		Jul 1998	Curtiba, Brazil	A Bullón	ADSAT
7		Aug 1998	Buenos Aires, Argentina	A Bullón	ADSAT
8		Oct 1998	Joao Pessoa, Brazil	A Bullón	ADSAT
9	NET '98—NeXt Millennium	Oct 1998	Andrews University, Berrien Springs, Michigan, USA	D Nelson	Americas, Europe, Africa, India, Asia, Australia
			1999		
10	ACTS 2000 (1)	Jan 1999	Manila, Philippines	M Finley	Pacific Rim
11	ACTS 2000 (2)	Mar 1999	Kumasi, Ghana	M Finley	Africa, Papua New Guinea
12	ACTS 2000 (3)	May 1999	São Paulo, Brazil	M Finley	ADSAT
13	La Red	Aug 1999	Miami, FL, USA	A Bullón	ADSAT
14	ACTS 2000 (4)	Sep 1999	Bucharest, Romania	M Finley	Europe
15	Amazing Facts	Oct 1999	New York, NY, USA	D Batchelor	North America, Europe, Africa, Australia
16		Oct 1999	Belém, Brazil	A Bullón	ADSAT
17	ACTS 2000 (5)	Nov 1999	Santiago, Chile	M Finley	ADSAT
18	NET '99	Nov 1999	Darmstadt, Germany	H Gerhardt	Europe
			2000		
19	ACTS 2000 (6)	Jan 2000	Madras, India	M Finley	No Broadcast
20	Jubilee 2000	Feb 2000	Rome, Italy	R Ianno	Europe
21	ACTS 2000 (7)	Mar 2000	Los Angeles, CA, USA	M Finley	North America
22	Holy Week	Apr 2000	Nova Friburgo, Brazil	A Bullón	ADSAT
23	Esperanza 2000	Apr 2000	São Paulo, Brazil	H Feyerabend	ADSAT, Europe, Portugal, VHS to Africa
24	Jesus 2000	May 2000	Sydney, Australia	G Yeoulden	Pacific Rim, Europe
25	Holy Week	May 2000	Lima, Peru	A Bullón	ADSAT
26	Pentecost 2000	Sep 2000	Port Elizabeth, South Africa	L Pollard	Africa
27	ACTS 2000 (8)	Oct 2000	Seoul, Korea	M Finley	Pacific Rim
28	Midnight Cry	Oct 2000	Chicago, IL, USA	K Cox	Americas
29	Jesus 2000	Oct 2000	Germany	G Yeoulden	Europe
30	Regards 2000	Nov 2000	France	T Lenoir	Europe, Africa
			2001		
31		Feb 2001	Havana, Cuba	A Bullón	ADSAT
32	ACTS 2000 (9)	Mar 2001	Jamaica	M Finley	ADSAT
33	Holy Week	Apr 2001	Nova Friburgo, Brazil	Pr Stina	ADSAT
34		Jun 2001	São Paulo, Brazil	J Viana	ADSAT
35	Christ 2000	Jun 2001	Tanzania	J Patzer	Africa
36	ACTS 2000 (10)	Jul 2001	Port Moresby, Papua New Guinea	M Finley	Pacific Rim
37	Take Charge of Your Life	Aug 2001	Australia	P Jacks	Pacific Rim
38	Peace to Live	Oct 2001	Portugal	J Carlos	Europe, Africa, ADSAT
39		Oct 2001	Guarulhos, Brazil	A Bullón	ADSAT, Europe
40	Christ 2001	Nov 2001	Romania	J Patzer	Europe
41	NET 2001	Nov 2001	Germany	M Mueller	Europe

			2002		
42	The Galilean	Feb 2002	Romania	L Cristescu	Europe
43		Feb 2002	Santo Domingo, Dominican Republic	A Bullón	ADSAT, Europe
44	Holy Week	Apr 2002	South America	A Bullón	ADSAT
45		Jun 2002	Trujillo, Peru	M Ferreira	ADSAT, Europe
46	REZ 10	Aug 2002	Australia	Youth	Pacific Rim
47		Oct 2002	Mexico	Youth - variety	ADSAT, Europe
48	Revelation Speaks Peace	Oct 2002	Montreal, Canada	H Feyerabend, S Boonstra	Americas
49		Oct 2002	Germany	Variety	Europe
50		Nov 2002	Switzerland	EUD Youth Series	Europe
51		Nov 2002	Washington, D.C., USA	A Bullón	North American Division, ADSAT
52	Visions for Life	Nov 2002	Yaounde, Cameroon	D Batchelor	Africa, India
53	Revive	Nov 2002	Campos, RJ, Brazil	A Bullón	Brazil, Europe
			2003		
54	A Season of Reconciliation	Feb 2003	Bucharest, Romania	N Butoi	Europe, Africa, Asia
55	Americas for Christ 2003	Mar 2003	Santo Domingo, Dominican Republic	J Patzer	ADSAT, Europe
56	A Man for All Time—the Incomparable Christ	Mar 2003	Orlando, FL, USA	M Finley	NAD
57	A Man for All Time	Apr 2003	Santo Domingo, Dominican Republic	M Finley	ADSAT
58	VOP: NET	Apr 2003	Columbia, SC, USA	L Melashenko	NAD, Pacific Rim
59		Apr 2003	Nova Friburgo , Brazil	Pr Montano	ADSAT, Europe
60		Jun 2003	La Paz, Bolivia	A Bullón	ADSAT, Europe
61	Hope for Our Troubled World	Aug 2003	Lusaka, Zambia	L Melashenko	Africa
62	La Red	Oct 2003	New York, NY, USA	A Bullón	ADSAT
63	Regard 2003: CAP Sur Jesus	Oct 2003	France	M Luthringer	Europe
64	Palabras de Vida y Esperanza	Oct 2003	Guatemala City, Guatemala	Various pastors	ADSAT, Americas
65	A New Revelation	Nov 2003	Seoul, Korea	D Batchelor	Korea,
66	Visions for Victory	Nov 2003	Aba, Nigeria	D Schneider	Africa
67	Revive	Nov 2003	South America	F Iglesias	ADSAT
			2004		
68	Evidence	Mar 2004	Bracknell, England	D Nelson	Europe, Africa
69		Mar 2004	Santa Cruz, Bolivia	M Rivero	ADSAT
70	Footsteps of Jesus	Apr 2004	Auckland, New Zealand	B Marchiano	Pacific Rim
71		Jul 2004	Caracas, Venezuela	M Finley	ADSAT/ADVENIR[†]
72	New Life—Hope for Today	Aug 2004	Kigali, Rwanda	M Finley	Africa
73		Sep 2004	La Paz, Bolivia	A Bullón	ADSAT
74	NET 2004—Experience the Power	Oct 2004	Baltimore, MD, USA	W Pierson	Americas
75	Link2Life	Oct 2004	Darstadt, Germany	S Sigg	Europe
76	Decubras	Nov 2004	Simi Valley, CA, USA	F Gonzalez	Americas
77		Nov 2004	São Paulo, Brazil	F Iglesia	ADSAT
78	Christ 2004	Nov 2004	São Paulo, Brazil	J Patzer	ADSAT
			2005		
79	Mind the Gap	Feb 2005	London, UK	D Nelson	Americas, Europe
80		Mar 2005	Kiev, Ukraine	M Finley	Europe
81	Prophecy Code	Mar 2005	Silver Spring, MD, USA	D Batchelor	Americas
82	Holy Week	Mar 2005	Inter-American Division		Americas
83		Apr 2005	Point Fortin, Trinidad	R Daniels	Americas
84	Seven Signs	Apr 2005	Forest Lake Academy, Florida	J Rojas	Americas

*ADSAT (Adventist Satellite) provided programming for the South American Division.
[†]ADVENIR provided programming for the South American Division.

Acknowledgments

Since this book focuses on miracles, it is obvious the primary acknowledgment rightly belongs to our Almighty God. By His divine action, He created the subject of this book. As I thought about the various miraculous experiences, organized the contents, made selections, and wrote these stories, my faith in God has been tremendously strengthened. I don't understand why God has allowed our family to share in Adventist Television Network (ATN) the way we have. It is humbling and inspiring, and I thank God for giving us the privilege of being associated with ATN and seeing what God is doing with this modern communication technology.

I am also grateful to the many people who have helped in various ways to bring this book into existence. Many of them hold heavy administrative roles, yet they made time to verify details and share their memories and stories of satellite evangelism.

I am indebted to my wonderful husband, Brad, director of ATN, who did extensive editing on the final draft of this manuscript. We've had the privilege of working together on so many projects through the years. Working together on *Miracle Factor,* however, was a special experience for which I am so thankful! I'm not sure this manuscript would have gotten finished without his loving support and encouragement and the hours we spent reviewing every detail.

My brother-in-law Greg started all this. He's a great brother-in-law, even though he bugged me for five years to write this book! Family is so very important, and the prayers of our parents, Wilf and Arlene Janot and Jack

Thorp, and my saintly grandmothers, along with those of many friends, have been tremendously important.

I owe Marcelo Vallado much for his patience, time, and diligence in verifying details from the numerous NET events he assisted and for helping me communicate with our Portuguese-speaking friends in Brazil. Williams and Sonete Costa's support has been so important. Thank you! And Herman Schreven's enthusiastic help and advice has been vital in shaping this book. I'm grateful and wish to thank him too.

Michelle Stotz and Pastor Royce Williams provided invaluable material from It Is Written (IIW).

I am grateful for the caring and interested support given by the Rutland Adventist church. Through the years, the families of our home church have prayed for us in our travels and ministry, supported our family, welcomed us home, and listened with interest to our stories and reports. Special thanks to Joan Kapinak for being willing to read and reread drafts of this manuscript and to offer helpful suggestions and encouragement.

Appreciation goes to my assistants, Loma Boyd and Kirsten Palipane. Loma helped by caring for our busy office and answering phones and emails in my absence. And Kirsten cheerfully combed through nearly thirty thousand emails, finding details for various stories featured in this book. I also much appreciate her keying and rekeying the manuscript, but her encouragement meant the most.

The lines "No man is an island; no man stands alone" are very true for ATN. God has worked through many, many individuals to establish and develop ATN. This global network comprises a large team, synergistically combining the resources of the church. Space does not permit me to mention everyone by name, but I wish to acknowledge and thank the following entities and each individual in the various organizations that make up this network for their encouragement and support and for allowing God to use them to advance His work.

Adventist administrators: This group of very dedicated, visionary, and gifted church leaders is seldom seen on ATN broadcasts. However, without their guidance and support, ATN wouldn't exist. They are the key leaders who guide ATN today. Pastor Robert Folkenberg was president of the world Adventist Church and took a leading role in organizing ATN. Pastor Jan Paulsen followed him as world Adventist Church president and continued to provide strong support and encouragement. Vice President Phil Follett was ATN's initial chairperson and worked tirelessly. At the time of the writing of this book, Vice President Ted Wilson chairs ATN, giving spiritual leadership. He has given particularly strong support for the development of the direct-to-home Hope channels. The world church treasurers and vice presidents and the presidents of the various global divisions, along with other administrative, departmental, and ministerial leaders, have also lent their support in many ways.

ATN staff: Since the very beginning of satellite NET evangelism, Carolyn Kujawa has faithfully served ATN as secretary to Phil Follett and then to Ted Wilson and at the same time to my husband, Brad, who is the director of ATN. Carolyn has cared for the mundane and tried to keep us in order and out of trouble. She has edited documents and dispensed counsel and has always been ready to jump cheerfully into solving an emergency for us. If ATN has a mother, it is Carolyn. She and all our past and current staff deserve a huge Thank you!

Several other organizations and the people they represent deserve acknowledgment too. ACN: The Adventist Church in North America through its Adventist Communication Network is the corporate "founding father" of ATN. ACN continues to work closely with ATN, which now provides the satellite broadcast service for ACN.

AMC: The Adventist Church in North America operates the Adventist Media Center in Simi Valley, California. AMC is the headquarters for many of the TV and radio ministries of the church. AMC and the various ministries have kindly given ATN access to the video resources of the church, thus providing the backbone of ATN/Hope Channel programming. Under ATN direction, Adventist Media Services (AMS) provides the scheduling service for Hope Channel broadcasts coming from California.

AMP: Adventist Media Productions functions under AMC. This organization, capably led by Warren Judd, has provided vital technical support for the conception and development of satellite NET evangelism. ATN wouldn't exist without the creative leadership of Warren and his AMP team. Today, AMP provides a wide range of production services for satellite evangelism and various ministries in the church. It also provides for ATN the ongoing broadcast service of the Hope Channel, Esperanza Channel, Hope Channel International, and Hope Channel—Europe.

ASI: The Adventist Laymen's Services and Industries organization of North America played a pivotal role in establishing ATN. Dan and Karen Houghton along with Denzil and Donna McNeilus have given creative ideas, enthusiasm, and strong encouragement to various ATN initiatives.

Church media centers: When satellite NET evangelism began in 1995, only two fully equipped Adventist Church TV production centers existed—AMC in Australia and AMC in California. Today, from Australia to Zambia, more than forty Adventist TV production centers are producing programs for ATN. Some of these centers are small; some, quite large. These centers represent several hundred individuals and tremendous creativity and dedication.

Other groups deserve acknowledgment too. Church members: Our brothers and sisters in Christ caught the vision of satellite NET evangelism, gave sacrificially to purchase and install equipment, did the hard work of preparing and following up satellite NET events, welcomed us when we and the production teams traveled to their lands, and are faithfully seeking to distribute Hope Channel.

Evangelists: How can people hear without a preacher? Satellite NET evangelism would not exist without evangelists who have a burden for this ministry and who have poured their life into proclaiming the Bible message creatively. Many of them have used the influence of their organizations to support the expansion of the network. (See the appendix for a list of all satellite NET evangelism events and speakers.)

Producers and directors: These talented individuals take the concepts of satellite NET evangelism and Adventist television and do their best to make it attractive on TV. More than two hundred individuals attended our first world Adventist TV producers' advisory. Colin Mead, director of production for Adventist Media Productions in California, deserves special recognition for his outstanding contribution, particularly in satellite NET evangelism. Colin has directed and/or produced scores of these global events, and I thank God for his ministry.

Satellite coordinators: Key to communication for all levels of church organization have been the satellite coordinators in each region. Church administrators, ministerial association leaders, communication directors, and personal ministries directors have filled this role. Other people serve as satellite coordinators in every geographic region of the world, through all levels of church organization, including the local church. Each of these individuals has worked hard to share news of NET events and ATN developments.

Technical support teams: A group of technical support individuals has provided immense support for the establishment and operation of the global ATN network. Pastor Doug Janssen pioneered this technical support work in NET '95 and continues today to support churches across North America. Errol Van Eck in South Africa has dedicated countless hours to writing manuals, troubleshooting, and helping in so many ways. Ian and Velma

Miller from Canada, Jorge Florencio in South America, Stefan Fraunberger and Lothar Klepp in Central Europe, David Gibbons in Australia, and many others lead teams that provide technical support to churches in large regions. We also thank each local church technical support team for all they do to ensure good reception on a local church basis.

Three Angels Broadcasting Network: This TV ministry supports the Adventist Church, which has freely supplied a great deal of programming to 3ABN. Through the years this ministry has been instrumental in bringing many to Jesus. Although not a formal part of ATN, 3ABN has played an important role in the development of ATN. 3ABN's influence has established confidence in full-time TV ministry—a foundation upon which ATN builds.

One of my favorite authors wrote an inspirational quote that sums up the holy boldness Seventh-day Adventists have had as they have worked to use satellite evangelism to spread the story of salvation: "God will have men who will venture anything and everything to save souls. Those who will not move until they can see every step of the way clearly before them will not be of advantage at this time to forward the truth of God. There must be workers now who will push ahead in the dark as well as in the light, and who will hold up bravely under discouragements and disappointed hopes, and yet work on with faith, with tears and patient hope, sowing beside all waters, trusting the Lord to bring the increase. God calls for men of nerve, of hope, faith, and endurance, to work to the point."[1]

[1]Ellen G. White, *Evangelism* (Hagerstown, Maryland.: Review and Herald, 1946), 63.

Photo Credits

Section I, page 28: Todd Gessle; page 35: Brad Thorp; pages 39, 40: Kurt Johnson; page 43: Warren Judd; page 49: David G. Gibbons; page 50: Marcelo Vallado; page 55: Marcelo Vallado; page 56 (both photos): It Is Written; page 64: Marcelo Vallado; page 66: Erlo Braun; page 70: Colin Mead; page 72: Robert Folkenberg; page 82: Marcelo Vallado; page 85: Warren Judd; page 92 (both photos): Gunter Koch; page 98: Kandus Thorp

Section II, page 103: Gunter Koch; page 107: Gunter Koch; page 110: Warren Judd; page 116: Wilton Costa; page 120 (top): Catherine Molina; page 120 (bottom): Wilton Costa; page 121: Kandus Thorp; page 124: Warren Judd; page 128: It Is Written; page 130: It Is Written; page 133: Royce Williams, It Is Written; page 146: It Is Written

Section III, page 148: Marcelo Vallado; page 155: Jorge Florencio; page 157: Brad Thorp; page 161: Mary Lane Anderson; page 163: It Is Written; page 165: Amazing Facts; page 166: Amazing Facts; page 169: Kandus Thorp; page 171: François Louw; page 173: Andre Brink; page 178: Dick Duerksen

If you enjoyed *Miracle Factor,* you'll enjoy these items as well:

Prophecies of Hope Bible Lessons

A brand-new set of 26 full-color, full-message lessons developed by *Gary Gibbs* of Hope TV and designed to be used in conjunction with Hope TV's evangelistic programming. The "fill-in-the-blanks" feature fits the busy lifestyle of most people today. Lessons include, "Prophecy's Superpowers," "Satan's Secret Strategy," "Death's Mystery Solved," "Modern Prophets," and more.

4333003484. US$5.99, Can$8.49/set. Also available as packs of 50 individual lessons for US$11.99, Can$16.49

Born to Preach

The inspirational autobiography of evangelist *Henry Feyerabend.* From the windswept prairies of his beloved Saskatchewan to the exotic tropical land of Brazil and back again—Henry's life saga spans many years and miles, countless signs of God's leading, and thrilling miracle after miracle!

0-8163-2086-1. Paperback.

US$14.99, Can$20.49.

Pursuing the Passion of Jesus

Dwight K. Nelson. An eye-opening look at Isaiah 58 that shows how loving the least—personal and practical ministry to those who suffer—helps you fulfill God's purpose for your life.

0-8163-2043-8. Paperback.

US$10.99, Can$14.99.

Order from your ABC by calling 1-800-765-6955, or get online and shop our virtual store at www.AdventistBookCenter.com.

• Read a chapter from your favorite book
• Order online
• Sign up for email notices on new products

Prices subject to change without notice.